THE SHEPPEY LIGHT RAILWAY

by Brian Hart

WILD SWAN PUBLICATIONS LTD.

A wayside corner of the 'Unknown Paradise' where whispering trees along leafy avenues greeted those who travelled to Leysdown on the Sheppey Light Railway to explore this Kentish island.
Author's collection

INTRODUCTION

Without exception, the branch railways of Kent were varied and colourful, each possessing a separate, identifiable character. Such a circumstance most likely came about as a result of the rivalry between the South Eastern Railway and the London, Chatham and Dover Railway. Between them, these companies created a network which basically remains intact to this day, criss-crossing the countryside in a fashion that was often more beneficial to their shareholders than the hapless travelling public.

Added to this historic framework around the turn of the century came the standard-gauge light railways, bringing with them even greater variance and interest to the intriguing story of rail transport in Kent. One of the most successful was the Sheppey Light Railway, conceived by the islanders in the 1890s and engineered by the well-known and revered Holman F. Stephens. He was responsible for many other light railways, not only in Kent, but right across the country.

Right from the outset, fortune smiled on this line which leisurely meandered its way across the gently undulating hills and bleak marshes of the island to the remote hamlet of Leysdown. The principal villages along the route, Minster and Eastchurch, as well as the scattered communities in between, suddenly found themselves on the railway map. As a result, great and confident hopes for the development and even entire transformation of the island were subsequently forthcoming. The initial demand for the services offered by this new line was so great, notably from the agricultural trade, that the branch soon relinquished its independent status to become absorbed into the South Eastern & Chatham Railway. This 'seal of approval' was, in every sense, a measure of the SE & CR's confidence in its future. Equally, it was as great a landmark as had been the line's inception. From this moment it was improved, enlarged and partly standardised. Even so, the Sheppey Light proudly clung onto its sense of individuality which, remarkably, it managed to retain for half a century.

For a dozen or so years, the light railway enjoyed the company of an electric tramway system which Sheerness and its outlying districts gained during Edwardian times. Combined, these ventures ably served the islanders and visitors who crowded aboard the swaying tramcars and into the quaint railway carriages. Throughout these years of prosperous growth and well-being it seemed that nothing would, or could, ever change matters for the worse. However, the appalling horrors of the Great War, together with its associated calamitous effects, rent the very fabric of society and heralded profound changes in social customs. These grim years, as well as the restless times that followed, took a heavy toll as economic depression overshadowed everything. Remarkably, the Sheppey Light managed to survive, prospering when other light railways faltered and eventually succumbed, as did parts of the long-established system constructed by the major companies which were quite ruthlessly pruned. However, it seems fate was yet awhile prepared to open another door just as one closed, enabling the line to adapt to fluctuating circumstances, the trains constantly running and maintaining its usefulness.

Matters were very different at the end of the Second World War. The odds against the railway's continuing survival were now stacked so high that its demise came fairly swiftly. This was brought about by the combined popularity of the motor car, the increasing availability of the local 'bus and the door-to-door convenience of the road van and lorry which ultimately drained the lifeblood of the line. In an age which looked towards increasing road transport as the utopian ideal, there was precious little hope left on the horizon for a relatively little-used eight-mile branch line leading to an undeveloped resort at the mouth of the Thames. Thus, it was allowed to go the way of so many lines during that post-war period, as well as those which subsequently suffered the consequences of even worse policies pursued throughout the 1960s.

Nowadays, there is almost nothing left to show where this particular light railway traced its way across the island. Perhaps the odd scattered remnant, here and there, evokes a distant memory and prompts a wistful daydream among older residents who can recall those happy, carefree childhood holidays spent at Leysdown. Or maybe today's younger generations, if they are of a mind to roam their local fields and meadows as we once did, might pause and wonder if they stumble upon some long-hidden, overgrown remains. Yet, in spite of its ultimate dismantling, it would be foolish to dismiss it as a failure, or a worthless undertaking. It was certainly neither, since it well and ably served its purpose throughout its fifty years existence. Rather it was we who failed it, than it which failed us.

Not since one visit in my childhood, in the 'fifties, had I been to the island, but the desire to see the place again presented itself following the completion of this book. I dared half-wonder whether any of the scenes depicted in the Edwardian postcard views might still exist in some quiet and undeveloped corners. Our trip, on a sunny Sunday in the summer of 1991, took us to a busy, crowded Leysdown, full of today's Londoners whose glossy status symbols were parked upon every worn verge and rutted patch of grass along the windswept foreshore. Its few narrow roads were bordered with bright and garish amusements, whilst 'take-aways' and stalls offering cheap knick-knacks to clutter the home, were perused by a seemingly aimless populace. Smothering the fields and meadows, which had once been almost the sole domain of sheep and marsh birds, marched a relentless sprawl of mobile homes, huts and shacks, giving the impression of a shanty town intent on forever expanding unhindered in all directions.

Modern, sweeping roads now cut a swathe across the open countryside, enabling all kinds of motor vehicles to spill out across the island from the not-too-distant London-Dover motorway. The wayside verges and hedgerows are now spattered with the usual oily, dusty grime as today's trippers pay more attention to the rear of the car in front than gaze askant to see the fallow fields and distant horizons. The visual pollution of hundreds of brightly-coloured metal boxes glinting in a summer landscape is something that is probably never contemplated, yet how harsh and inharmonious it looks. Worse still, these hostile tarmac highways with their associated roundabouts and junctions, necessitating huge illuminated signs and rows of sodium lights, remain a constant eyesore. Long after their users have made their weary way home, these sterile arteries remain ablaze with artificial light where only a night-time scavenging fox runs, or tiny hedgehog scuttles, across the hard, unfriendly ground that was once a quiet

'When the sea goes out it leaves a wide stretch of shallow water on the sands, and a bright busy sky is reflected cheerfully into the shallows below.' — Arthur Lewis.
Author's collection

field. I often find myself wondering if those who sweat and curse, cooped up in their cars on the long trek home, truly enjoy a better day at Leysdown than those who dozed contentedly on the gently swaying homeward train sixty years ago? Is this the reality of the romantic-looking isle that I glimpsed three years ago from a hilltop near Whitstable, its gentle form distant in the purplish dusk, across the lazy Swale, as a fiery-amber sun slipped beneath a late-autumn horizon?

So-called progress has, perhaps, been a little kinder to Eastchurch, but only by its relative absence. Moments later we found ourselves in Minster, yet so many houses now border the roads that the distinction between these places is imperceptible. In 1936, Arthur Mee spoke of Minster as once being the 'marvel of the Isle of Sheppey', praising this old place 'set in a silver sea'.

But he found ugliness even half a century ago and roundly condemned the builders of 'bungalows and petty things'. Alas, I can only conclude that time has not been kind to Minster, nor the island which it commands, and I left with uneasy feelings of sorrow and remorse. However, such appears to be the way of our world these days.

My only intention in compiling this book has been to try and record for posterity something of the history of this remarkable railway. I have likewise been motivated in my desire to present some of the enchanting scenes, beautifully captured by the numerous photographers who have wandered through this wayside district over the years. Perhaps because these aspects have so totally disappeared there is all the more reason to attempt a sympathetic presentation here in what I hope will be something to treasure and look back upon. If, after reading this book, it can be put down with feelings of warmth and pleasure, accompanied with a moment's reflection such as: 'Yes, it was a worthwhile venture and how lovely it all once looked' then I shall have achieved all I ever set out to do.

Brian Hart
Uckfield
Sussex
1992

This book is warmly dedicated to
REG RANDELL
in recognition of all his help and
encouragement over the years.

CHAPTER ONE

ISLE OF SHEEP

WHEREAS the Isles of Grain and Thanet have long-since ceased to be proper islands, Sheppey remains truly separate from the mainland of Kent. In reality it is made up of three islands, but nowadays the distinction is barely perceptible, even with the aid of a map. The largest of the three is Sheppey itself, which contains within its boundaries all the towns and industries which have housed and sustained the island communities for generations. In the south eastern corner is the Isle of Harty, with Elmley Island to the west. Both border the Swale which flows between Whitstable Bay in the east and the River Medway in the west. The island is approximately eleven miles from end to end and about four miles in breadth. The highest point is at Minster, the land being mostly London clay which, at some places, extends to a depth of around 500 ft. This clay is exposed at the eastern end where the ruddy brown cliffs at Warden Bay are under constant attack by the sea.

It acquired its name, perhaps not unexpectedly, from the animals which have been successfully reared for centuries, stretching back as far as the Anglo-Saxons and probably beyond. Blessed with a temperate climate and fertile soil, the rich grazing pastures have brought local farmers widespread acclaim for 'Sheppey Mutton', once highly prized for its excellent quality. Elsewhere, crops such as wheat, barley, oats, beans and turnips provided a valuable trade with the London markets, while its proximity to the Thames facilitated the transportation of produce by river barge and ship to the capital with relative ease. A correspondent in the *Gentlemen's Magazine* of September 1860 spoke of:

> 'Well cultivated fields, with handsome timber in the hedges, forming often shady lanes that would delight the painter, are characteristic of the north of the island. Much of the land is occupied as market gardens, or for growing to contract valuable crops (as canary or mustard) for the London seedsmen. Indeed, Sheppey wherever arable land is found, is emphatically the region of high farming, and no one but a wealthy tenant can long hold land there. Consequently the farms are yearly getting larger and larger, and holdings of 1,000 acres are not uncommon. As a natural result, the hedges and water-courses are all kept in the best order, the fields are clean, and every farm office testifies to the well-to-do condition of the agriculturalist. Steam machinery appears every here and there; the fences and gates and vehicles are kept so freshly painted as to seem always new, and the well-fed horses are ordinarily decorated with coloured fringes to their harness.'

Six hundred years ago the Swale was a much busier and more important waterway, for it formed the regular passageway into the River Thames. Ships from the English Channel entered the River Stour at Sandwich before sailing up the narrow Wantsum which separated the Isle of Thanet from the rest of Kent. Entering the sea once more at Reculver, they continued past Whitstable and into the Swale, joining the Medway near Chetney Marshes. Crossing the estuary, they traversed the Colemouth and Yantlet Creeks which divided the Isle of Grain from the Hundred of Hoo, before reaching the Thames. The wharves and settlements along the way, Harty and Queenborough on the Isle of Sheppey, Tong and Milton on the opposite shore, were once important places but their status diminished over the centuries. By the end of the nineteenth century the Swale was still navigable for vessels up to 200 tons, but most of the craft which traversed these sheltered waters were associated with the flourishing oyster and fishing industries.

Access to Sheppey was via three ferries which served each separate island. At the eastern end the Harty Ferry provided a useful connection between land, the distance across the water being almost a mile at high tide. The toll in 1890 was 4d each way or sixpence after sunset. At that time it was operated by Mr George Marshall, licensee of 'The Ferry House Inn' on the isle. Harty was once isolated from the rest of Sheppey by the Cable Creek, but this was drained over a century ago. In 1881 its population stood at 157 while the small school catered for just 34 mixed pupils. The Harty Ferry is featured in Walter Jerrold's inspiring 1907 account, *Highways & Byways in Kent:*

> 'Leaving Faversham by Davington Hill we get, from the small village of Oare, a good view of the "crick" by which boats reach the town. West in the marsh is Luddenham church. Going on to Harty Ferry we pass across the marsh where many sheep pasture, and reach the embankment by which the land has been reclaimed. The ferry house is at the other side of the Swale on the Isle of Sheppey, and a patient wait will at length be rewarded by the arrival of the boat across the three-quarters of a mile of high-tide water. At low tide there are innumerable gulls, curlews and other birds, and these the wayfarer may well have time to watch if delayed as I have been for over an hour by thunder, hail and wind, that made the return of the boat impossible, a squall which washed boats and barges from their moorings, and even swept the gulls like large snow flakes down the wind. It was August, and the sun was shining brightly but an hour after the country had been shadowed by grey-edged clouds of inky blackness.'

Separating Harty from the neighbouring island of Elmley is Windmill Creek, or Crog Dick as it was once more commonly and curiously termed. Elmley gives the impression of even greater bleakness, its windswept marshes leading down to the Swale where idle water, disturbed by a stiff breeze, splashes about the inlets and islets of this dispiriting place. In spite of the wind-borne sounds of modern trade and the cries of the marsh birds, this lonely and remote spot seems wholly detached from the outside world. The scene is quite often vividly reminiscent of those fictitious realms of Dickens, whose wonderment and enthusiasm for the Cliffe Marshes in the Hundred of Hoo, so inspired his creative genius. Indeed, a fertile imagination might half expect to see at any moment a shackled convict rise from the reeds before fleeing towards a grisly end in the treacherous quagmires beyond.

At one time it was possible to take the Elmley Ferry to reach the mainland, just half a mile across the narrowing Swale. On the other side the land soon rises amidst the familiar orchards of the garden county around Tong where an abundance of fragrant blossom still brings springtime cheer to the hearts of Kentish folk. This ferry, however, ceased operating years ago, although it lasted long enough to appear upon the 1930s Ordnance Survey maps.

The parish of Elmley once enjoyed a populace slightly greater than that of Harty, around 200 souls in 1881, whilst the local school boasted an attendance of 52. Murray's *Hand Book for Kent* published in 1892 states that 'Elmley is almost entirely marshland, but it has a Portland cement factory', whilst Black's guide speaks of 'a significant air of business and prosperity'. Just across the water, at about the narrowest part of the Swale, is Ridham Dock where a network of sidings and even an aerial ropeway were built.

Continuing westwards along the Swale the King's Ferry crossing is soon reached. Originally this too was, of course, a traditionally operated ferry, but a bridge soon replaced it in the industrious nineteenth century and nowadays a thoroughly modern structure with a lifting span creates a landmark for miles around. The provision of a permanent bridge was arguably the greatest improvement of all for Sheppey. Construction began in the late 1850s with the building of the Sheerness & Sittingbourne Railway which opened in July 1860. For the first few years the branch was worked by the London, Chatham and Dover Railway but, not surprisingly, the company and its line were eventually absorbed into the LC & DR's system. Interestingly enough, the rival South Eastern Railway had, some years before, announced its intention to serve Sheppey. In 1845 shareholders were informed that plans were afoot to build a new line through North Kent, with a branch from Milton to Sheerness. Although this scheme came to nought, as late as August 1856 ovations were still being made to the SER, seeking an extension of their railway from Gravesend to Sheerness. The SER directors quite indifferently referred the request to their traffic committees for consideration, but eventually declined contributing a penny towards the scheme, although they did reply that they'd be willing to work the line if constructed. As a result of their disinterest, the East Kent Railway, which later became the LC & DR, were smart in taking advantage and moved into this territory. By doing so they were eventually able to establish rival routes between the Kentish ports and the capital.

The first King's Ferry bridge is described thus in Murray's 1892 guide:

> 'The line from Sittingbourne, which is joined by the line direct from Chatham at the Sittingbourne Middle Junction, passes between the church of Milton, and mound of Tong Castle on the east, and Iwade on the west, and at $3\frac{1}{2}$ miles crosses the Swale, which separates Sheppey from the mainland, on an iron girder-bridge, resting on brick piers, in 7 fathom water. It is near the site of the ancient King's Ferry (which it has superseded), and is so arranged as to afford a road for pedestrians and carriages, whilst in the centre is a drawbridge, to allow vessels to pass through.'

Beyond the bridge, the navigation continues through Long Reach before almost doubling back upon itself to where is found the most ancient settlement on the island. This is Queenborough, named in honour of the wife of Edward III who erected a castle here in the 14th century. Nowadays, very little of this structure remains, most of the surviving remnants having thoughtlessly been destroyed with the construction of the railway. The castle well, which reached a tremendous depth of some 270 feet, was utilised by the LC & DR. Around 1868 the company constructed a well house whereby, with the aid of steam power, it was able to pump up copious quantities. It was also used for the town's supply and was rightly seen as a great bonus since fresh water was scant throughout the island, other sources being quite brackish and unwholesome. Indeed, Sheppey seems to have been extremely fortunate in not being troubled by 'marsh-ague', a

A glimpse of Edwardian Queenborough along the road that led the visitor from the quayside to the railway station. *Author's collection*

The 'huddled and muddled' streets of Blue Town, Sheerness, which contrasted so markedly with Sheppey's lonely, windswept rural districts.
Author's collection

form of malaria common in marshlands between the 16th and 18th centuries which plagued the neighbouring wetlands across the Medway in the Hundred of Hoo. *Kelly's Directory* in 1892 concluded that Sheppey could justifiably claim to be a fortunate spot:

> 'The climate is salubrious and the land fertile. The death rate seldom exceeds 14 in the thousand, showing the unusual healthiness of the locality.'

At Queenborough the LC & DR constructed a branch line, approximately one mile in length, to a new pier on the Medway and facing the Isle of Grain. This project was carried out partly because problems were being experienced at Sheerness with insufficient draught. More importantly, however, it was seen as a means of developing trade outside the Continental Traffic Agreement of 1865. This arrangement had been drawn up in the vague hope of ending the squabbling between the two rival Kent railway companies whereby continental receipts from all ports between Margate and Hastings would be pooled and divided. Both the SER and LC & DR grew to detest the obligation and mistrusted each other. As a result, this led to some quite remarkable and spectacular schemes being planned and sometimes carried out during the following two decades.

The Queenborough Pier branch opened on 15th May 1876 with a service to Flushing [nowadays Vlissingen]. The SER was quite infuriated by this move and quickly retaliated. Just weeks after the opening of Queenborough Pier, they sent instructions to their chief engineer, Francis Brady, to come up with a rival project. In a little over a year he presented 'a scheme of my own' to his directors whereby a nominally independent company, the 'Hundred of Hoo Railway' was launched, financially sustained and eventually absorbed by the SER in 1882. At arguably the bleakest and by far the most barren spots in Kent the SER built its terminal pier and station bordering the banks of the Medway, upon the Isle of Grain and immediately opposite Queenborough. Imperiously named 'Port Victoria' after the reigning monarch, it was truly one of the most astounding ventures in the history of railways in Southern England.

A few months before the opening of this new SER port, the LC & DR suffered a setback when Queenborough Pier was ravaged by fire in May 1882. Nevertheless, it turned out to be a blessing in disguise for the opportunity thereby arose to provide even better facilities than its rival, as well as extending further into deeper water with a pier some 650 feet in length.

The coming of the railway undoubtedly enabled Queenborough to flourish and some considerable industries were established. Seemingly inexhaustible amounts of London clay allowed pottery manufacture to thrive, whilst iron pyrites were also commonplace, enabling Queenborough to begin the production of brimstone (sulphur) and copperas, used to create among other things sulphuric acid. Lime burning was another important industry and especially useful locally in cement manufacture and the dressing of the heavy clay soil.

A little beyond Queenborough, the road and railway pass through West Minster where the Sheppey Gas Company set up its works. Gas was a great advance and convenience, even though its manufacture was unfortunately often odious and offensive.

Rural Warden at the eastern end of the isle and a scene of long ago, for all the cottages save the farthest have since tumbled over the eroded cliffs.
Collection Martin Hawkins

The terminal station of the S & SR was situated near to Sheerness Dockyard, convenient for the railway company, but less so for the town's inhabitants who faced a walk of about a mile. There was little incentive to change matters but, with the opening of Port Victoria, the need to remedy the situation became readily apparent. Apart from establishing its own service to Flushing, the SER began to steal much of the LC & DR's Sheerness traffic. Evidence of this appears in the contemporary guide books which instruct the traveller to take the train to Port Victoria 'whence they may be free to avail themselves of a short and expeditious crossing to Sheerness'. Since the SER charged by the mile and their route from London to Sheerness via Port Victoria clipped a good twelve miles off the journey, they were able to offer cheaper fares than their rivals. Passengers using the LC & DR route were also normally obliged to make a number of changes at stations along the route, thus adding further disincentives and disadvantage. Although reaction to Port Victoria had been swift, with the LC & DR opening a new spur line and station at 'Sheerness-on-Sea' in June 1883, the SER route was often the preferred choice, especially in the season.

At the time of the establishment of Queenborough in the 14th century, Sheerness is said to have been 'nothing more than a mere swamp'. During the mid-1600s a fort was erected as a strategic defensive measure against the marauding Dutch who captured it and retained it for a while under their Admiral De Ruyter. Eventually retaken and refortified, the base grew as docks were laid out with wharves, smitheries, sail-loft and rigging houses being built to sustain a naval headquarters. The settlement originally comprised four separate districts – Blue Town, Banks Town, Marine Town and Mile Town, the last three incorporated within Sheerness-on-Sea. *Kelly's Directory* of 1892 comments:

'Sheerness-on-Sea is the modern part of Sheerness proper, from which it is separated by a moat, crossed by two bridges giving access to the pier and Dockyard railway station; it is built near the beach at the estuary of the Thames on the northern shore of the Isle of Sheppey and is rising in popularity as a resort for visitors and pleasure residents: it has a fine esplanade, extending from Garrison Fort to Cheyney Rock, forming a long and pleasant promenade. The London, Chatham and Dover Railway Co. have a new station close to the beach. About a mile east the cliffs of London clay begin. The Thames here is about five miles broad and the floating Nore light at the mouth of the river marks the position of the Nore sands and is a prominent beacon.'

Continuing around the coast, Minster-on-Sea, as it has sometimes been glowingly termed, lies about three miles on. Here there are bracing and very pleasant clifftop walks which were recommended for their views by the Victorian guide books:

'In front is the Thames with its myriad vessels. Sheerness spreads out below, and landward extends a wide sweep of rich corn and pastureland through which winds the Medway. The scene is perhaps as striking, from the variety of objects it comprises, as any in Kent, and is not likely to be forgotten.'

About six miles further, Warden Bay is reached, followed by Leysdown, the easternmost settlement in the island. From here it is possible to walk along the coastline for about two miles to stand upon the extremity known as Shell Ness. Here, at the mouth of the Swale, the view extends across the Oaze to Seasalter and Whitstable. Upon these waters the Whitstable oyster and fishing fleets have hauled in their catches for generations in a locality that has found the sea both friend and enemy. Sustainer and destroyer, the sea remains ultimately all-powerful over man's defences against its ravaging might. Yet, without its presence almost all reason for existence here would be gone, as well as the need to develop harbours and railways.

With the establishment of docks, industries and a thriving farming business, the Sittingbourne and Sheerness Railway became an integral part of the island's economy. However, such benefits and opportunities extended only to the western edge. It is therefore not surprising that the scene was set in the late 1890s for the promotion of a new line to serve the centre and eastern side which would link together the communities along the way.

CHAPTER TWO

RAILWAY PROMOTION

By the mid-1890s there was already an identifiable need for a second railway in Sheppey and its creation came about with the juxtaposition of a numbers of factors.

Almost all the roads in the area were primitive tracks, the clay soil breaking down into a powdery dust in summer, whilst slippery, puddled furrows in winter considerably hindered the transportation of produce and commodities. The farming communities were anxious to see improvements, as were the inhabitants of the villages and scattered parishes along the way. At that time there were two carriers operating from Eastchurch, John Pankhurst and William Grant, who both provided a daily van except on Sundays. Minster, with a population of 1,600, was the largest settlement with an interest in having the railway, followed by Eastchurch at 900 and Leysdown at 200.

Had the land been divided into smallholdings then it is less likely that a railway would have been constructed. Indeed, any ovations to the LC & DR would have almost certainly been brushed aside. However, many of Sheppey's fertile acres belonged to influential landowners, including Lord Harris of Belmont Park, Faversham and the millionaire Robert Holford. These gentlemen were well aware of the need to improve matters on their estates, so they approached a business colleague and friend, Lord Medway, to see what he had to say concerning his involvement in the recent opening of a railway in the Weald of Kent to Cranbrook and Hawkhurst.

By far the most significant factor in the securement of a railway through the district to Leysdown was unquestionably the passing of the Light Railways Act of 1896. This important piece of legislation facilitated the construction of minor railways which could be laid down without the need for heavy and costly engineering works where projects would have otherwise faltered on a financial criterion. The act opened the way for numerous projects throughout the country, some more successful than others, but in general terms the light railways were warmly received as a useful and beneficial asset.

The progress of the act had been studiously followed with great interest by the Sheppey Board of Guardians and it seems that as soon as the royal seal had been affixed, action was taken. Upon hearing the news, Mr A.W. Howe, hurried along to the board, telling them: 'Now is the time to get a light railway for Sheppey'. A colleague, Mr John Copland was equally enthusiastic, saying: 'I shall be glad to do all I can to get one' and from then onwards, it is related, he worked quietly and diligently towards that goal.

The catalyst in the Sheppey scheme appears to have been a young trainee engineer, Holman Stephens, who until relatively recently had been working on the Cranbrook & Paddock Wood Railway under Edward Seaton. Seaton was the engineer employed by the SER to construct this latest addition to their system which had taken many years to secure. Had the Light Railway Act been passed twenty years earlier then the inhabitants and landowners of the High Weald might not have waited for so long. However, this line was constructed to orthodox methods and was not a light railway in any sense whatsoever. Nevertheless, the project did enable the youthful Stephens to gain useful knowledge and experience in civil engineering and a training which stood him in good stead throughout the following years.

With the completion and opening of the railway as far as Hawkhurst in the autumn of 1893, Stephens bided his time in Cranbrook, hoping to find further work on the anticipated extension of this new line to Tenterden and maybe Appledore. In the event the proposals evaporated, leaving the luckless Stephens scratching around for any engineering work wherever he could find it. Fortunately for him, his associations with the C & PWR and the SER companies had given him the chance to meet some of the directors, as well as Lord Medway at the celebratory luncheon at Hawkhurst. Lord Medway, alias John Stewart Gathorne-Hardy, was heir to the Earl of Cranbrook, and both father and son had been institutional in securing the C & PWR. Lord Medway had also been the MP for Mid-Kent from 1885 to 1892, so he was capable of exerting considerable influence. It is difficult to imagine the ambitious Stephens *not* having made his presence known to his lordship who agreed to do everything he could to find him a position within the SER. Even though this hope came to nothing, another door opened as revealed in a letter from Holman Stephens to his father:

> Tonbridge, Kent.
> 29th November 1896
>
> My Dear Dah,
> I have a letter of introduction from Lord Medway to Lord Harris "re" a proposed line in the Isle of Sheppey. You know so much better than I do how to manage these sort of things; how shall I address Lord Harris?
> I write "My dear Lord Medway" because I know him, but I don't know Lord H. Shall I say "Sir" !! or "My Lord"?
> With best love to you both,
> Your affectionate son.

Perhaps it was at this point that the Sheppey scheme was begun and the following year saw the establishment of a company with the intention of running a direct line south from Queenborough, through the Neats Court and South Lees Marshes, directly to Leysdown. By this time Stephens had already established his 'Engineer's Office' at Salford Terrace in Tonbridge where other light railways were being organised. Upon printed notepaper headed 'Sheppey Railway', he took charge of this latest project, the line being plotted out and promoted by a company formed in 1895 entitled the 'Light Railway Syndicate Ltd'.

Following a number of visits to the island to inspect the route of the proposed new line, Stephens and his colleagues were evidently mindful of the possibilities offered by the terminal point at Leysdown. Here there was a good beach within a reasonable travelling distance from London. Accordingly, Stephens produced his engineering plans for a line which required very little excavation since the land was almost level, running along the northern borders of the marshes in the centre of the island. The estimate for the railway was put at £43,852 and preliminary advertisements were placed in the *Sheerness Guardian*. Shortly afterwards Mr John Copland, representing the Rural District Council, approached the promoters to advise them quite firmly that their chosen route was certainly not the most advantageous. A suggestion was made that the junction with the LC & DR should be positioned north of Queenborough station, facing in the opposite direction. This arrangement would allow the railway to run near Sheerness before passing much closer to

The rugged beauty of Minster cliffs which border the wide mouth of the River Thames and where the soft clay hills forever remain at the mercy of the North Sea. *Author's collection*

Minster. From here it should continue in a south-easterly direction before joining up with their original alignment near Eastchurch. Stephens evidently approved of the superior plan, even though greater earthworks were required with an eventual additional expenditure of £8,571 being incurred. Fortunately for the Sheppey company the landowners directly affected by the deviation welcomed the chance of having the railway. Since the price of wheat had collapsed, most of these once-cultivated pastures had been allowed to remain fallow, whilst land values were similarly at rock-bottom. With a railway, perishable produce such as fruit and salad crops, as well as root vegetables, could be quickly and easily transported to the mainland markets, thereby reviving local fortune.

In due course a public enquiry was held on the afternoon of Friday, 21st April 1898, at Queenborough Town Hall. The meeting was crowded with people from all over the island and there followed much debate and interest in the proceedings. The revised proposals for a new line serving Queenborough and the villages along the route to Leysdown were put before the Light Railway Commissioners. Apart from the advantages of serving the agriculturalists, it was argued that the ordinary inhabitants of the island would gain significantly, whilst at the Leysdown Estate 'there was every prospect of making it a flourishing seaside spot'. It was anticipated that the LC & DR would do everything possible to accommodate the light railway at Queenborough whereby passengers could change trains to the advantage of both companies. It also transpired that a hotel at Leysdown was planned, but details and size were not discussed. Mr Edward Peterson, the solicitor to the company, then rose to speak. It might be mentioned that Peterson practised in Cranbrook where he first made Stephens' acquaintance, hence his involvement. He said he'd been over the route which was fairly flat and although he wasn't an engineer it appeared to be easy railway country. Almost all the landowners affected by the revised route had given written consent of their favour, the last but one having done so that very morning. It emerged that some opposition

Two rare glimpses of Queenborough station in Edwardian days, showing the terminus of the Sheppey Light Railway. The clutter of enamelled advertising signs was once such a common sight, whilst the Sheppey Light goods brake van in the bay is worthy of note.
Author's collection

had been encountered towards the original route, but now there was almost complete unanimity over the revised proposals.

Holman Stephens then gave evidence and produced his plans for the commissioners to inspect. The line would be standard gauge and built to such a degree as to carry main line trucks and passenger trains at 'any reasonable speed the commissioners chose to sanction'. Since direct communication into the LC & DR's Queenborough station had been refused, a revised plan proposed a separate platform which had raised costs only a little. Stephens considered that his railway would encourage people to move out of Sheerness to Minster which was, in his opinion, 'much higher and prettier'. He also claimed that a large proportion of land there had already been purchased by a building society for residential purposes.

At the request of the Earl of Jersey who presided at the enquiry, Stephens then gave a description of the route:

> 'The line at present will have a junction on the east side of the Queenborough goods station; then run north-east towards a house called Sheppey Court, where it will cross a road leading from Sheerness to Minster. We hope to have a gate-house and a station there. 'The line will run under the hill and cross the road at a point below Harp's Farm. The train can be seen coming within half-a-mile within each corner. A station will be on the road near Borstal Hall, this being the nearest spot to the village of Minster. We then go on to Brambledown, New Hook, Stamford Hill, White House, New Rides and terminate at a point close to Leysdown coast-guard station. The line will be laid to enable the ordinary traffic to pass over. I may add that we intend to provide shelter at all the stations.'

Mr Penney, from the Sheerness & Isle of Sheppey Chamber of Commerce, was then allowed to speak, at which he suggested that the line should commence not at Queenborough, but at the Dockyard station. Stephens replied:

> 'If we adopt the suggestion, we should have to run our trains up the High Street, and I hardly like to have the boldness to propose such a scheme. It would be a very excellent thing indeed if we could do it, but we should only be allowed to run goods trucks and horse boxes through the street up till about eleven in the day.'

Mr Penney explained his reasoning, arguing that if facilities were opened up at Sheerness Pier, then people coming by the Port Victoria route would have the opportunity of going to Leysdown. Perhaps having had his suspicions aroused, Stephens then enquired: 'May I ask if you are acting on behalf of the South Eastern Railway Company', whereupon Mr Penney insisted he was only representing the tradesmen and had no interest in any particular railway company. Mr Stephens then explained that the junction had to be at Queenborough for the sake of the goods traffic.

Mr Comley, for the LC & DR, informed the hearing that so long as his company could be assured that their goods business would not be interfered with at Queenborough, then no objections to the light railway proposals would be tabled.

Elaborating on other matters, Stephens declared that the intended speed would be 35mph, adding that whenever there was an excursion to Leysdown it was advisable to get the passengers there as speedily as possible. He hoped the speed would not be reduced by the Board of Trade. He also spoke of his intention to have gate-houses at the crossings so that they could be attended by the wives of the men who would be employed on the line.

Mr Barton Hallett then spoke of his ambition to transform Leysdown, adding that he had recently entered into a contract for developing the estate as a seaside resort. He considered the locality offered excellent opportunities 'far in advance of Southend and many other places along the coast'.

Speaking for Sheerness, Mr Edward Brightman, the chairman of the Urban District Council, commented that a light railway would be of great advantage to the locality. He considered the diverted route would increase the number of passengers from the town to other parts of the island. He also thought the residents at Sheerness would be glad to have a tramway through the town but, for the moment, the council wouldn't want to do anything which might injure the present scheme.

Mr Herbert Berry, from the Chamber of Commerce, thought it was generally accepted that the new line would be of tremendous advantage to the rural districts, but he failed to see how it could benefit Sheerness unless Mr Penney's suggestion of linking it to the Dockyard station was adopted. He couldn't see why a feeder line through Blue Town to the station should be opposed by the LC & DR. Indeed, he claimed, a number of other gentlemen thought this was a good proposal.

Support for the railway wasn't entirely unanimous since one farmer, Mr T. Goodwin, complained that his holding would be bisected and that he would lose a large pond. However, after a brief consultation with Mr Stephens, at which a compromise was reached, he withdrew his objection and duly added his signature to the agreement.

In summing up, Lord Jersey considered it was evident that there was a desire in the district for a light railway and the Commissioners would recommend the Board of Trade to issue an order for its construction. Since there was no real objection to the diversion of the railway, he declined insisting on more public notice which could result in the project being unnecessarily delayed for as much as a year. Regarding the interests of Sheerness, he noted that the gentlemen did not oppose the scheme, but merely desired the town to be included. In his considered opinion he thought it might be achieved in due course and therefore recommended the application be granted.

Even with matters proceeding as hastily as possible, it was not until a year later, on 3rd May 1899, that the Sheppey Light Railway Company received authorisation to proceed with the construction of the line. The order from the commissioners, with amendments from the Board of Trade, specified that rails weighing at least 60 lbs per yard should be laid, a limit of 14 tons axle weight would be imposed and that the maximum speed must not exceed 25 miles an hour. This must have disappointed Stephens whose hopes for a normal running speed of 35 mph were dashed. Trains would also be required to slow down to 10 mph at every level crossing, whilst any locomotives with tenders running in reverse should be restricted to an overall speed not exceeding 15 mph. The track, signalling and telecommunications would have to comply to the satisfaction of the BoT before permission for opening would be granted, as would the platforms and access. However, the order confirmed that the company was under no obligation to 'provide shelters or conveniences at any station or stopping place'. Fares were not to exceed 3d a mile 1st class, 2d a mile 2nd class and a penny a mile 3rd class. Steam was the authorised power, although the order included provisions in case electric traction should be introduced at a later date, subject to BoT requirements. Such clauses may well have been included given the fact that proposals were already being widely aired for an electric tramway system around the island with, hopefully, the two enterprises eventually being linked. For the moment, though, all thoughts were concentrated on an orthodox railway operated by steam locomotives.

CHAPTER THREE

'SUCCESS TO THE SHEPPEY LIGHT'

THE prospect of opening up the island for development must have brought some cheer to the farmers and landowners who were concerned by the state of the agricultural market at the time. Even though the harvest of 1899 proved to be no less bountiful, there was widespread gloom as the price of wheat had collapsed to such a degree that its production was stated to be 'hardly remunerative'.

Since railways represented commerce, wealth-creation and the betterment of living standards, the gradual material evidence of the new line must surely have been encouraging for the islanders. Proposals for new lines were always eagerly reported, especially where it affected the local area. During that summer, news came of a scheme to link Sittingbourne directly with Maidstone via the Stockbury valley, whilst another envisaged a direct route from Faversham to Lenham. The *Sheerness Times* thought the former proposal worthwhile since it would benefit the island, but dismissed the latter as 'of no use'. In January 1900 the paper commented:

> 'The Sheppey Light Railway, when first projected, was hardly taken seriously in some quarters, but it will soon be an accomplished fact. A start has been made, and as the line is expected to progress at the rate of a mile per month, there is every reason to believe that before the new century appears the railway will be in working order. The effect of the line on the prospect of rural Sheppey will be watched with interest. We hope there are better times in store for the hardly-hit agricultural community. If the development of Leysdown as a watering place is one result of the light railway, the farmers will find a market close at hand for some of their produce.'

To celebrate the commencement of the new line an 'inaugural supper' was held on the evening of Wednesday, 10th January, at the 'Halfway House Inn'. Around thirty guests sat down to a good spread upon the table, which was followed by the loyal toast and the singing of the National Anthem. After toasting 'Success to the Light Railway', the chairman expressed his deep satisfaction over the start of building. In response, Mr Bert Mason, chief engineer of the SLR, told the assembly that the contractors, Messrs. William Rigby & Co., would be proceeding with the work as rapidly as possible. In his estimation the line should be complete and operational within nine to twelve months time. Another toast, 'Success to the SE and C & DR' was coupled with best wishes to Mr H. B. Stanford on his promotion to station superintendent at Ramsgate. Stepping into his shoes at Queenborough as station master was Mr J. Howland, so glasses were raised to wish him well, with the hope that he might also be given charge of the new line. Mr Farnell Brown then rose to say that he'd taken a great interest in the trade of Sheppey, as well as the light railway. He firmly believed that Leysdown was destined to become one of the finest watering places on the Kent Coast. Finally, the evening was rounded off with toasts to the British and Colonial troops currently fighting the Boers in South Africa, followed by a rousing sing-song including 'The Soldiers of the Queen', 'Auld Lang Syne', and another enthusiastic rendition of the National Anthem.

Little time was wasted in getting on with the work. The route was soon stumped out, while gangs of men under the foremanship of Mr Brotherton began the minor earthworks to carry the railway. Local people watched the progress with much interest, no doubt looking forward to the day when they could avail themselves of a ride upon the new line. However, this didn't mean that the railway contractors could do just as they pleased, as revealed in the *Sheerness Times* of 24th March:

> 'The Sheppey Light Railway cuts across the pathway between Brecknock Hill and the Cemetery. This is one of the prettiest walks in the neighbourhood of Sheerness and it is very desirable that the rights of the public should in no way be prejudiced by the construction of the light railway. We notice that stiles have been fitted this week by the contractor to enable the public to pass over the wire fencing, but they appear to us to be totally inadequate for the purpose. Certainly a third step is needed to render them passable with ease, but it would be far more convenient if small gates were fitted, the same as at the end of Birdcage Walk. The Minster Parish Council might take the matter up.'

The business of travelling or sending goods was extremely important to the Isle of Sheppey, so it is hardly surprising that the subject received good coverage in the local press. Sheerness people had often felt that they had been at the mercy of the LC & DR which had the monopoly on the island's railway services. The building of the Hundred of Hoo Railway to Port Victoria in the 1880s had promised to change all that and, for a while, there seems to have been a general sense of satisfaction that the SER had come to the rescue of the town. However, the Port Victoria route did, of course, entail a ferry journey across the mouth of the Medway and this was often subject to the weather or the SER's whims. Following the working agreement between the SER and LC & DR in 1899, hopes of greater improvements in the island's services remained unrealised, indeed there seems to have been even less incentive than before. The sporadic nature of the Sheerness-Port Victoria-London service was a reason for frequent complaint, often in quite exasperated terms. In May 1900 the SE & CR reintroduced the train service to Port Victoria [the winter timetable normally saw trains terminated halfway at Sharnal Street] but Sheerness residents were told that the ferry wouldn't be operating until the following month. This caused widespread bewilderment, not to mention annoyance, and there was much wonderment as to who should want to go to Port Victoria and not continue to Sheerness? When the steamboat did return on the service, there continued to be mutterings of discontent that it would probably be taken off at the end of the season. Patronage of the service in winter, however, must have been extremely low, so the SE & CR cannot have been acting entirely without justification.

A significant development in the island's transport history took place at this time with the establishment of the 'County of Kent Electrical Power Distribution Co. Ltd'. Through this company an application was made for a Light Railway Order for the construction of an electric tramway system. It was proposed to commence in West Street, close to the Sheerness Pier and Dockyard station, before proceeding along the High Street where a branch would run off along Marine Parade as far as Cheyney Rock. From the High Street the route would continue along the Halfway House Road, crossing the light railway at the site designated for Sheerness East station. At a 'T' junction beyond the railway, the westerly route would run along the road to Queenborough station, whilst in the opposite direction the tramway would continue to Minster, crossing the light railway for a second time. Initially there were few objections to the tramway system, but it wasn't long before the light railway company began to worry about the threat posed by the trams.

Of particular concern was the likelihood of the spurs to Queenborough and Minster stealing prospective passengers away from their trains. By mounting vigorous opposition to the tram tracks crossing the line, they were successful in preventing a comprehensive system being authorised and the unfortunate tram company had to be content with just $2\frac{1}{2}$ miles within Sheerness. It was a victory for the Sheppey Light, but that was all, for the general public would undeniably have been better served by the trams.

With the tramway having suffered a temporary but severe setback, all attention was focused upon the new railway. The *Sheerness Times* reported in September that the trains should begin running in about five months and went on to express the hope that the parishes of Minster, Eastchurch and Leysdown might still be connected up to Sheerness by both rail and tram. Along the route the contractors were making good progress and the first sections of track were already in place. To assist with operations William Rigby hired a 'Terrier' 0–6–0T locomotive, No. 671 formerly named *Wapping*, from the London, Brighton & South Coast Railway at £2 per day.

In November the SLR Co. was remonstrated for positioning the gate posts so that the highway was narrowed where the line crossed the Halfway House to Minster road [eventually East Minster level crossing]. The council considered them to be especially dangerous at night to persons travelling along the road and suggested that the contractor be ordered immediately to move them.

By the New Year of 1901, claims were being made that the railway would soon be ready for public opening throughout. Already some goods trips as far as Eastchurch were possible as reported by Mr Horspool at a meeting of the Sheerness Rural District Council. He revealed with some satisfaction that in the first week of January sixteen tons of coal had been transported to Eastchurch station and delivered in the space of three quarters of an hour. He considered this a very good beginning and vastly different treatment from that which Sheerness tradesmen were currently receiving. Why, he exclaimed, they often had to wait days for goods weighing just a few hundredweight.

While the benefits to tradesmen and agriculturalists were becoming daily apparent, the aspirations for Leysdown began to seem less certain. The *Sheerness Times*, on 5th January 1901 remarked:

'The development of Leysdown as a watering place is not likely to follow so closely in the wake of the Light Railway as at one time

Queenborough station, looking towards Sheerness in the first few years of the opening of the light railway. It appears that a train from Leysdown has just arrived, hauled by one of the 'Sondes' class 2–4–0 tanks which initially worked the service. The goods shed can be seen at the end of the up platform, whilst across the line is the elevated signal box and a splitting junction signal.

Collection Reg Randell

Sheerness East station with a train bound for Queenborough waiting alongside the platform. The ornate pole near the station building supported the overhead feeder for the Sheerness Electric Tramway Company whose tram depot was nearby. *Collection Reg Randell*

seemed probable. The scheme is said to have been abandoned for the present, but there are many who believe it will come to pass before many years have passed.'

A further interesting insight into the detraction from the original optimistic plans came with a letter from Rigby to the Rural District Council. Instead of providing watchmen's huts at the numerous points where the line crossed roadways, he asked whether it would be acceptable to substitute cattle guards 'until traffic increased on the railway'. The council asked for a sketch of the guards and eventually a compromise was reached as to the safe operation of these crossings.

By April it was reported that the work was 'being pushed forward at a rapid rate' with the opening expected on 1st June. The opportunity was taken to reveal that the SE & CR were going to lease the railway for five years.

From his Tonbridge office, Stephens wrote to the Board of Trade on 13th May, informing them that the Sheppey Light Railway would be ready for opening in four weeks time. However, the works could not be completed by that deadline and he was obliged to send a second notice to the Board on 10th June, stating that everything should be ready within three days. The BoT appointed Major Pringle to carry out the inspection and he subsequently wrote to Stephens proposing Friday, 21st. This proved to be satisfactory and Major Pringle's report, which provides a most interesting insight into the light railway as originally laid down, reads as follows:

> I have the honour to report for the information of the Board of Trade, that in compliance with the instructions contained in your Minute of the 12th inst., I made an inspection today of the Sheppey Light Railway.
>
> This light railway, constructed under the Order of 1898, commences at Queenborough Station on the Sittingbourne & Sheerness Branch of the SE & C Railway, and traverses the parishes of Minster, Eastchurch and Leysdown within the limits of deviation shown on the deposited plans and diversion. It terminates near the Leysdown Coastguard Station.
>
> The total length of route is 8 miles 52 chains. The railway has a single line throughout except at three points, Queenborough, Eastchurch & Leysdown where there are loops, but none of these, at present, are anticipated to be used for passing passengers trains.
>
> Land has been purchased for a single line only. The width at formation level is 15 feet, the gauge being 4' 8½". Between double lines there is a space of six feet, and at a height of 2 feet 6 inches above rail level there is a clear space of 2' 6" between the sides of the widest carriages & any fixed work.
>
> The railway is substantially fenced on both sides with seven lines of wire, the top wire being 4 feet above the ground. The straining brackets are fixed in oak posts situated at furlong intervals.
>
> No difficulty has been experienced with the drainage.
>
> The steepest gradient has an inclination of 1 in 70 and extends for a distance of 38 chains. The two sharpest curves have a radius of 14 chains and 20 chains respectively.
>
> The permanent way consists of part worn (SE & C) steel bullhead rails weighing not less than 70 lbs per yard, in lengths of from 24 to 30 feet. They are jointed by fish plates weighing 30 lbs per pair with four bolts, and rest on cast iron chairs each weighing not less than 30 lbs. The chairs are secured by two spikes & trenails to half round, adzed & creosoted sleepers each 9' x 10" x 5". These are spaced from 2' 10" to 3' 0" apart. The bottom ballast is stated to consist of 9" of clinkers covered by 4" of sand shingle. I thought the ballast was short in quantity outside the ends of the sleepers.
>
> The earthwork is very light, the deepest cutting and highest bank does not appear to exceed 10 feet in depth or height respectively.
>
> The soil is a description of loamy clay.
>
> There are no bridges, viaducts, tunnels or culverts on the railway.
>
> No turntable has been provided, and the traffic I am informed is to be worked by tank engines.
>
> Level Crossings. There are 5 footpath, 31 occupation, and 11 public road level crossings shown on the table.
>
> Of the occupation level crossings, one (at 2 mile 24 chns) is provided with cattle guards instead of the usual side gates, so as to permit the development of a building estate. This concession by the company appears to argue recognition or dedication on their part of the crossing as a public one.
>
> Of the 11 public road crossings, four are provided with gates in accordance with the Order, and 5 with cattleguards, and I was informed that they were shown in error as public road crossings.
>
> I suggest therefore that the table be returned for correction as regards the entries against these three level crossings.
>
> The gates for the four public roads are 16 feet in width, and conform with the Order as regards closing across the railway. In three instances when open for railway traffic they also close across the road on each side of the railway. In the case of the public road

at 1 mile 37 chains, the gates open in the same direction and meet across the road on one side of the railway only. I see no objection to this.

None of the road authorities concerned were represented on the occasion of my inspection and I understand they have expressed themselves satisfied with the arrangements.

The cattleguards are sufficiently explained in the drawing furnished by the Company. The grids are however of wood, and can scarcely prove durable, nor in my opinion are they so effective as narrower grids would be of angle iron. They appear however to have been accepted without demur by the residents.

At three of the public road level crossings where gates exist, a gatekeeper's hut has been erected. In this hut a bell is rung to give warning of the approach of a train, but some special bell code must be adopted, by which signals to the various huts can be distinguished.

The country traversed is very open & unfenced and in all cases there is an excellent view of the public road crossings to anyone approaching them on the road from either direction, and I think all the requirements of safety have been complied with. There are two staff sections on the line, viz. Queenborough to Eastchurch & thence to Leysdown.

Stations. There are 6 stations or platforms for the use of passengers as follows:-

1. Queenborough. There is a single platform line on the east side of the up main platform, and a loop which will be mainly used for goods traffic. There is a signal for approaching & leaving the station, and the facing points are provided with locking bars & bolts and detectors are provided. The points and signals are worked from a covered ground frame containing 8 levers. The interlocking is correct.

2. East Sheerness Station – at 1 mile 38 chains.

3. Minster Station – at 3 miles 8 chains.

The arrangement at these two stations is similar. There is a single line and platform, the latter is provided with a shelter & urinal. There is a siding controlled by a ground frame with two levers, properly interlocked. The frame can only be used by inserting the train staff of the section. No signals.

4. East Minster Platform – at 2 miles 44 chains. There is only a single line & short platform with a small shelter at this place. No signals.

5. Eastchurch Station – at 5 miles 45 chains. Here there is a loop line signalled for each direction, with a single platform provided with the usual shelter, and a goods siding. It is a train staff station, but although provided with a loop, is not at present, with only one platform, suitable for a passing place for passenger trains. If therefore, at any future time, it should habitually be used as a passing place for such trains a second platform would appear to be necessary. At each end of the loop there is a ground frame controlling the points and signal at that end, but there are requirements necessary to complete the interlocking.

6. Leysdown Station – at this terminus there is one platform with a larger shelter than elsewhere. There is a loop line and goods siding & loading bank. The points and entrance & exit signals

The truly rustic charm of East Minster-on-Sea where the bare minimum of facilities was provided. This is looking towards Sheerness East soon after opening.
Collection Reg Randell

Minster-on-Sea station, looking towards Leysdown, and the very epitome of what constituted a station, according to H. F. Stephens. This very early view shows what appears to be a tour of inspection by bowler-hatted gentlemen and workers upon a platelayers' pump trolley.
Collection Reg Randell

are controlled from a ground frame containing 6 levers properly interlocked.

Farm Sidings. There are four of these, at 3 miles 78 chains; 4 miles 71 chns; 6 miles 49 chns & 7 miles 6 chns respectively. The siding in each case accommodates two or three wagons and the points are controlled by a ground frame with two levers unlocked by the train staff. In each case the arrangements are satisfactory, except that in one instance the points are too close to a public road crossing, but the shunting will, I understand, be inconsiderable.

I make the following requirements:-
1. Many of the keys had fallen out, apparently from shrinkage and the line requires to be carefully keyed up throughout.
2. Various point connecting rods were lying about & should be fixed.
3. A small diagram should be supplied for the ground frame at Queenborough.
4. The platform at East Minster requires to be completed, the fencing at the back of the platform to be erected & lamps to be supplied.
5. At Eastchurch in the ground frame at the Sheerness end of the station Nos. 2 & 4 levers must interlock. No. 2 lever in this frame must lock Nos. 1 & 2 levers in the ground frame at the Leysdown end. This may temporarily be done by a wire lock. The wire lock at present existing between the two ground frames must be made to be operative as regards No. 2 lever in the frame at the Leysdown end before the line is used.
6. All the signal wires require adjusting so that the semaphores give a correct signal.
7. Within 6 weeks the wire lock or locks between the two ground frames at Leysdown must be replaced by rod locks.

Subject to the fulfilment of these requirements, and to the remarks on the passing of passenger trains at Eastchurch, I can recommend the Board of Trade to grant a certificate for the use of the light railway for passenger traffic under the train staff & ticket system.

I attach an undertaking by the Company as regards the working of the light railway.

I have the honour to be etc.,
J. W. Pringle, Maj. R. E.

It would appear that Stephens soon had the BoT requirements attended to, for on 29th June he wrote to them saying:

'Sir,
I beg to acknowledge your communication of 27th inst. & to inform you that Major Pringle's requirements have been complied with, with the exception of requirement No. 5 're' interlocking at Eastchurch Station. In this case the material is upon the ground & work is proceeding, the requirements will be finished it is estimated at least by Tuesday evening 2nd prox.

I have therefore to ask you to assist this small undertaking.'

Stephens' patience was tested over the next few weeks as it became evident that the line would still not be completed in time for an opening during July. Apart from the Board of Trade's list of outstanding works, the Urban District Council were concerned over the condition of Parsonage Lane, a rough trackway leading up to Eastchurch Station. William Rigby, the line's contractor, offered £50 towards the making up of this private road, but the council considered he should contribute double that amount.

Around that time, Kent County Council passed a new byelaw and, although it wasn't specifically intended to apply to the expected rush of daytrippers from the London suburbs to Leysdown, it was an attempt to calm down more excitable individuals. It rendered 'Noisy excursionists, blowing upon horns, or using any noisy instruments, or singing loudly to the annoyance of residents, liable to a penalty of £2 for each offence'!

During the last week of July there was a detectable sense of excitement in the island caused by the impending opening. The local paper expressed the hope that the line would fulfil expectations and bring about a new era of prosperity for the scattered communities. Details of the train service were made

The completed terminus at Leysdown. The building differed from those at Eastchurch, Minster and Sheerness, not only by being larger, but also most noticeably in the altered angle of the platform awning.
Collection Reg Randell

available, but there was some disappointment, especially among the farmers, that there was no early train from Leysdown which would enable them to reach Queenborough in time to catch the 8.45am from Sheerness.

Thursday, 1st August 1901, was a day for looking firmly towards a new future for the Isle of Sheppey and an account of the events that day duly appeared in the *Sheerness Times*:

OPENING OF THE SHEPPEY LIGHT RAILWAY.
The First Train starts amidst cheering and a Salute of Fog Signals.
The Sheppey Light Railway is now an accomplished fact. Whether it will bring about all the prosperity to rural Sheppey that has been predicted remains to be seen, but there can be no doubt that it will be a great convenience to the residents, who are now brought into communication with the railway system of the United Kingdom by means of the South Eastern & Chatham Company's line.

'The first train started from Queenborough at 9.05 on Thursday morning, and a goodly gathering assembled on the bridge which crosses the railway to witness its departure, while not a few took their seats for the initial voyage. The train was made up of six coaches – first and third class, there being no second class on the line – and a luggage van. It was drawn by one of the small locomotives, which has been allotted for regular duty upon the line.

The party of guests, noticeably all male, assembled at Leysdown station to commemorate the opening of the line.
Collection Peter Harding

Mr Howland, station-master at Queenborough, had gaily decorated the station with flags in honour of the auspicious event. Two or three officials made the first journey – Mr Smith, Assistant Superintendent of the SE & CR Company and Mr Durrant, Superintendent for the Faversham District accompanying whom was Alderman W. Pannell, of Queenborough who retired from the Company's service a few years since. Several local agriculturalists made the first journey, including Mr T. Clifford of Neat's Court, whilst the Union Officials were represented by Mr G. Bligh. Precisely to time, the passengers having taken their seats, the train steamed out of the station amidst hearty cheers, the waving of handkerchiefs, and the firing of fog signals, which had been placed along the line. All along the route bunting was liberally displayed on the farms and also at the stations at Sheerness East, Minster, Eastchurch, and Leysdown. There were several passengers waiting at Sheerness East, and on the arrival of the train at Minster, Mr Charles Ingleton JP and a number of residents were in waiting to welcome the first passenger train and to proceed in it to the terminus. Mr Thomas Horspool, who had made quite a brave show with bunting, met the train at Eastchurch, and at Leysdown Mr C. A. Till and other residents were present to greet the passengers by the pioneer train. Altogether it was a memorable day for Sheppey.

'A number of passengers met at the "Rose & Crown", Leysdown, and toasted 'Success to the Sheppey Light Railway'. A second train conveyed to Leysdown a number of South Eastern and Chatham Railway officials, including Mr Thompson, superintendent of the line; Mr Wallis, goods superintendent; and Mr Barker, locomotive superintendent. The officials, together with several gentlemen who had been connected with the construction of the line, afterwards lunched at the Royal Hotel, Sheerness, to celebrate the opening of the route.

'Mr S. Salmon, manager of Abbott and Co's, Boot Stores, 37 High Street, Mile Town, presented each passenger who travelled by the first train with a souvenir card with the times of arrival and departure of the trains.

'The route is through some of the best scenery in Sheppey.

'The luncheon that Mr Copland proposed giving on the opening day of the Light Railway was, at the request of the Directors of the SE & CR, postponed till the 9th, as they were unable to attend on the 1st. A special train will leave Victoria at 10.55 and arrive at Queenborough at 12.08. It will leave there at 12.13 and Sheerness East shortly after for the guests, and then after going to Leysdown will return to Sheerness East. The luncheon will be at the Co-operative Hall, Sheerness at 2.15.'

On the following day a regular service began, but a rare and special treat for those less fortunate was undoubtedly the highlight of the day when the children from the Union Workhouse were taken for a trip from Minster to Leysdown. The outing was paid for by Mrs Ingleton and her sister. It was reported that the children greatly enjoyed the ride, whilst on arrival at Leysdown they were 'regaled with lemonade and cake by Mrs Ingleton'. Mr Charles Ingleton accompanied the happy trippers and 'did all in his power to make the outing a success'.

The news of the opening of this latest addition to the railway system seems to have reached many ears, for over the Bank Holiday the trains were packed with visitors:

'The new Light Railway could not have been opened at a time when opportunities were more favourable for making it popular as a means

The end of the line at Leysdown showing the railway not long after completion and the starting signal at the end of the platform.
Collection Reg Randell

of transit to the other end of the island. The holiday on Monday induced hundreds to take advantage of the facilities offered for a trip to Leysdown, which, to many was a place existing only in name before. In all, no less than 1,770 tickets were issued on the line that day, the main point of departure being Sheerness East, where the platform was thronged with passengers for each train. The prettiness of the route, through fields of newly-cut corn and under the hills of Minster and the high ground of Eastchurch was generally admitted, some who were familiar with the villages being delighted with the new prospect afforded by a view of the localities from the route taken by the Light Railway. The beach at Leysdown presented quite a lively appearance. Of course Leysdown has only its natural attractions at present – chief of which is a fine sandy beach, with a grand view of the sea in front and pretty rural scenery behind. A splendid view, when the atmosphere is clear, is obtainable of the Kent Coast between Whitstable and Margate, while there is a constant panorama of passing ships bound for or departing from Old Father Thames. In course of time, if the anticipated development of this portion of Sheppey takes place, amusements will follow. The "raid" made on the Light Railway on the previous Thursday showed the necessity of additional provision being made to meet the creature wants of visitors to the "new watering place", many having to return hungry. But fortunately enterprise was not lacking. Mr Marsh Pierson, on Saturday, erected a large tent on a piece of spare ground at the side of the clean and neatly kept coastguard houses, within five minutes walk of the railway terminus, and provided teas for visitors – a convenience which has been greatly appreciated. Several visitors have also turned their efforts in the direction of catering for visitors at their houses.

'Some delay occurred in the arrival and departure of the last train, due, it is stated, to the engine going off the line at Queenborough. Some Eastchurch passengers, tired of waiting, wended their way homeward on foot.'

'Sheppey Cliffs were very popular with both visitors and residents on Monday. Seldom, if ever before, has such a large number of pleasure-seekers been seen on the cliffs, the favourite spots being near Constitution Hill and the "Royal Oak", although not a few were to be seen between East End Lane and Hensbrook, while the proximity of Warden to the Leysdown terminus of the Sheppey Light Railway induced many to stroll along the seashore from Leysdown Beach to the high ground at Warden, which is certainly one of the prettiest spots in Sheppey. The tide being up all the afternoon, the visitors saw the cliffs under the best possible auspices, and were delighted with their attractions. East End Lane was thronged with visitors, some driving up in traps from Sheerness, others walking from the Minster Station of the Light Railway, but the majority "footing" it along the sea-shore from Cheyney Rock. A few "natives" might have been seen boiling water pic-nic fashion for tea on the beach, and there was also a small party encamped for the holidays in a tent pitched on a suitable piece of ground halfway down the cliffs, opposite the point where the pathway leads into Minster.'

Holman Stephens must have enjoyed a sense of satisfaction and pride at the conclusion of his latest project. The Sheppey Light Railway was one of his more successful, but this may have been due to the fact that it was eventually absorbed into the SE & CR rather than remaining part of his scattered private empire of light railways. However, he contentedly wrote to his father on the 8th August:

Managing Director's Office,
Tonbridge.

My Dear Dah,
    Many thanks for your postcard. I am very glad to hear that you and Mam have again got to a place which you like so well and which does you so much good.
    I suppose Port Isaac is full of visitors and I have no doubt but that you are having grand weather.
    My little Sheppey Railway was opened for traffic on 1st Aug. but it is too early yet to say how the traffic will turn out.
    The SE & C Rly are working the line so that I have not much to do with the arrangements as I am only Engineer.
    The Rother Valley traffic is increasing well and so is the Chichester traffic. We are not affected by Coal or Labour troubles as our undertakings are so small.
    Hoping to see you both soon and with much love to both,
    I remain, Your affectionate son.

A week later, on Friday 16th August, the grand luncheon was held at the Co-operative Hall in Sheerness for nearly 160 guests to officially celebrate the opening. The guests were told to assemble at Sheerness East station at 12.15 for a ride to Leysdown upon a special train. At the terminus, a short stay enabled Mr Hider to take a photograph of all the smartly-dressed gentlemen lined up along the platform and track. It was a perfectly beautiful day with fine, dry weather which allowed the island to look its best. On returning to Sheerness East a number of traps were ready to convey the group to the luncheon. Notable guests from the SE & CR were Cosmo Bonsor, chairman; Vincent Hill, general manager; and Charles Sheath, secretary. Col. Boughey represented the Light Railway Commission, whilst the chief guests from the SLR Co. were Holman Stephens, engineer; William Rigby, contractor; and Edward Peterson, secretary.

Following grace, John Copland, clerk to the Sheppey Board of Guardians and host to the occasion, rose to speak amidst applause and cheers. Having given the loyal toast, he pointed to the large banner stretched out across their heads which read 'SUCCESS TO THE SHEPPEY LIGHT RAILWAY' and spoke of his satisfaction that all difficulties had been overcome. Bearing in mind the company present, John Copland then, surprisingly and rather tactlessly, continued with an attack on the original scheme as laid down by Stephens and said: 'What stupid people engineers sometimes are'. He reminded the gathering that they had 'proposed to take the line through the wretched southern marshes of Sheppey where nobody lived and nobody wanted to live!' It was, he asserted, 'solely due to the action of his Board that the line was now running through some of the most fertile lands in Sheppey' [applause].

Speaking for the Light Railway Commission, Colonel Boughey believed the right route had been chosen and he felt certain that it would benefit the island. He considered that it might be some time before traffic would build up, but hoped 'it would not be long before the line would be connected with another of the "children" of the Light Railway Commission – a tramway to Sheerness'.

Cosmo Bonsor then rose, amidst much applause, to speak on behalf of the SE & CR upon a number of railway matters affecting other parts of the island. Turning to the light railway, he expressed his delight at its promotion and successful conclusion since he believed it would 'act as a feeder and be of assistance to the great railway' – a remark which probably caused a few wry smiles. He considered that without the union between the SER and LC & DR, there would have been no light railway for Sheppey, since one company or other would have opposed it. In summing up he assured the assembly that the SE & CR would do all it could to serve the island and the irksome questions over the Swale bridge and the extension of a spur from their line into the dockyard would be readily addressed [applause].

Mr A. W. Howe then asked the gentlemen to raise their glasses to John Copland, 'for he has done more than anyone in securing the line to Leysdown'. In reply, Mr Copland said he was getting old and had lost the power of blushing, or he certainly would have blushed at the undeserved remark of Mr Howe. Nevertheless, it had been a pleasure for him, being a Sheerness man from infancy, to assist in the procurement of the railway, and also the tramway which was on its way.

Having sung 'God Save the King', the guests departed in time to catch the special train to London, no doubt satisfied that this corner of Kent and the SE & CR's system had taken a major stride into the twentieth century.

CHAPTER FOUR

PALMY DAYS

FOLLOWING the completion of the Sheppey contract, the men employed by Rigby were soon dispatched to other projects while outstanding works were quickly finished. The Rural District Council were still arguing with Rigby over the condition of the road leading up to Eastchurch station. The council brusquely told him they could not possibly accept his offer of £50 and demanded, once again, £100. Rigby responded by offering £80 before finally relenting and handing over the full amount, at which councillor Till somewhat ungratefully remarked: 'I should think so too, – he ought to have sent more'. Once the road had been completed, it was proposed to take it over as a public highway. The local press couldn't resist poking fun at the pompous and incongruous name which was then put forward:

'EASTCHURCH: A high-sounding title has been given to the approach to the Eastchurch Light Railway Station. Hitherto it has been known as Parsonage Lane, but this designation has now given place to "St George's Avenue and Riviera Drive"!'

The condition of the roadway at most of the level crossings was also causing concern, so much so that a memorial was presented by ratepayers and cyclists who sought a speedy remedy. The rails were apparently above the level of the road, while only loose gravel and clinker was laid on each side. They suggested a proper stone kerbing should be put down. Other people were more worried about the cattle guards in place of proper gates and felt these were a danger to children. However, the council decided that since Rigby was still responsible for the railway for another six months, they should at least give the works a fair trial.

With the fuss and celebrations out of the way, the everyday business of operating the line began. There were four trains each way, seven days a week, with the first departure from Queenborough at 9.05am. The journey took 35 minutes for the 8½ mile run to the seaside terminus – a rather lax timetable to say the least. After a twenty minute wait at Leysdown, during which time the engine ran round its train, the leisurely pace back to Queenborough resumed. Worked on the staff and ticket principle, it was operated as two sections, the staff for Queenborough – Eastchurch being a triangular brass bar painted red, while a circular green one was used for Eastchurch – Leysdown.

At the beginning of October the timetable was altered for the reasons given in the *Sheerness Times*:

'Only two trains are running to and from Leysdown daily during the present month but the service of four trains daily is maintained between Eastchurch and Queenborough. The times, however, have been altered, a train running earlier in the day to meet the generally expressed wish of the leading residents that a train should run from the island in connection with the 8.45am train from Sheerness. The timetable provides for a goods and passenger train to leave

The crew in charge of 2–4–0T No. 518, formerly *Sondes*, make last minute adjustments in the bay at Queenborough before departure for Leysdown.
Collection Dave Gilbert

Queenborough at 7 o'clock, returning from Eastchurch at 8.18am, Minster 8.30am and Sheerness East at 8.39am, arriving at Queenborough at 8.45am. The SE & CR announce that after October 31st Leysdown Station will be closed for passenger traffic until April 1st.'

Locomotives known to have worked the line for the first few years were three tank engines of which a total of six had originally been constructed for the LC & DR in 1858. Built as four-coupled bogie saddle tanks, they proved to be a dismal failure, so much so that they were all taken apart in 1865. However, the entire class was virtually reconstructed as conventional 2–4–0s and in this form they proved more reliable. Over the years they were reboilered and underwent further improvements and following the formation of the SE & CR the class was renumbered thus:

LC & DR No.	Name	SE & CR No.
59	Sondes	518*
60	Sittingbourne	519
61	Crampton	520*
62	Lake	521
63	Faversham	522
64	Chatham	523*

*[known to have worked the Sheppey Light Railway]

In his incomparable series on locomotive history, Don Bradley relates that 518 and 523 were sent to work on the Isle of Sheppey in 1901, whilst photographic evidence confirms that 520 also worked the light railway. These engines were impeccably cared for by the men at Sheerness shed. In addition to painting the coupling rods a striking bright red, it appears that every rivet and item of brasswork was highly polished. Another locomotive, a member of the *Aeolus* or Kirtley 'S' class, was similarly dispatched to assist with the service. This was No.533, formerly *Comus*, a 2–4–0T which, despite its age and condition, was similarly well-treated. *Comus*, was an equally interesting engine, built in 1861, but undergoing rebuilding in 1873 and again in 1886. During its lifetime it had been loaned out in 1883 to assist the contractor building the LC & DR's Maidstone to Ashford extension.

The coaching stock was improved soon after opening with the introduction of an ex-LC & DR 3-coach vestibuled set, as described by a correspondent writing for the *Sheerness Times* in January 1902:

'For the past month a corridor train has been running on the Sheppey Light Railway between Queenborough and Eastchurch. The cars are arranged longitudinally, and are cushioned, travelling for third class passengers being very comfortable. The object in running corridor cars is to render the issue of tickets more convenient. The guard of the train now passes from car to car between stations to issue tickets without risk of injury or exposure to the weather – a vast improvement on the system in vogue when the ordinary carriages were used and the guard had to walk along the footboard from compartment to compartment while the train was in motion to issue the tickets. The passenger traffic, we understand, is very limited just at present, but no doubt there will be a considerable increase when the proposed electric trams run from the Fountain Hotel to Sheerness East Station thus bringing rural Sheppey and Sheerness into direct communication.'

Throughout the winter the section to Leysdown remained closed to passengers, an understandable position in view of the yet unfulfilled prophecies of development. Such action may have been resented by those who lived at Leysdown and Warden, but at least there was hope of prosperous times ahead, unlike the unfortunate inhabitants of Elmley who had just lost their livelihood:

'ELMLEY'S DISMAL FUTURE:
The sad news concerning the Island of Elmley, communicated to the Sheppey Board of Guardians on Wednesday by the Rev. R. B. Barber, will be received with general regret. Few of the inhabitants of Sheerness have visited this remote parish, – which suffered seriously from the flood of 29th November 1897, but many may have noticed the smoke arising from the stack of chimneys at the Elmley cement works when crossing the Swale bridge in the train. The works have been closed, the employees and their families are leaving the island, and the village threatens to become, to use the words of the worthy rector, "a howling wilderness". The whole population of the island is not likely to number more than half a dozen families when the exodus is complete.'

The cause of the demise of the cement industry was blamed on 'German competition', whilst the little school, which once boasted 52 pupils, appeared quite doomed. Many of the families moved into Sheerness, whilst others left the area for good.

For Sheppey in general though, it appeared that as soon as one door closed another opened, thanks solely to the light railway. In February 1902 a new livestock market was established adjacent to Eastchurch station and to celebrate the occasion a small luncheon was staged. Local councillor Mr Howe asserted his belief that farmers would henceforth send their livestock into Sheppey via the light railway, whilst purchasers from all over the district would come flocking in to buy. Mr Horspool of the market committee said he'd resided on the island for nearly 18 years and had often heard people say it was 'useless going to Sheppey since there is no railroad for travellers either in or out'.

Kirtley 'S' Class No. 533, formerly *Comus*, which worked the Sheppey Light during the first years of opening.
Collection John Kite

Mr Charles Ingleton then harkened back to the days 'when old Sheppeyites, many of those present, could go back to the days when rural Sheppey was one of the most isolated places in creation'. He added: 'During the past twelve months Sheppey has become better known by the introduction of the light railway. Visitors have come who at one time never dreamed there was such a place as Sheppey. No one can deny that it will be the means of developing Sheppey' [applause].

The sight of the trains, either three passenger carriages, a rake of trucks, or the mixed runs, was becoming familiar to those who lived and worked in the area. They were accustomed to the lonesome sounds associated with marshes and skyscapes, the wind in the bent trees and grasses, the bleating of sheep, the twittering of unseen skylarks in summer or the cry of gulls in the bare winter fields and now there was another facet to rural life in Sheppey. Whereas the humble clock on the mantelpiece, or the strike of a 'grandfather' in the hall or parlour of the more affluent, had brought a sense of regularity to the day, the railway now reinforced this orderliness. To some, the passing of the local train became a useful reminder of the hour, a time to rise from bed, or lay down tools, or perhaps put on the potatoes for the evening meal. The railways more than anything else introduced, for good or bad, an awareness of the pace of life which had previously been left to the church clock. However, it was often prudent to use the passing of trains merely as a guide, for rarely were they precisely to time and occasionally they failed to turn up at all. Luckless travellers were frequently stranded at desolate stations, as was the case on 9th February 1902:

'ENGINE OFF THE LINE:
On Sunday evening last the engine employed on the Sheppey Light Railway got off the line at Queenborough station. A telephone message was sent to Eastchurch station, giving intimation that the

train due at 6.56pm would not arrive until about 12.30am. This was very unfortunate for some passengers who wished to return at 7.03pm to travel to London by the 8.20pm train from Queenborough. Some others who intended returning to Sheerness East by rail had to walk back to Sheerness.'

Had this irksome incident taken place a year later then the hapless passengers bound for Sheerness would have been able to jump on a tram for the last lap of their wearisome trek homewards.

In the spring of 1902 Mr George Ramuz, a land agent, commenced with the disposal of a large number of plots close to Eastchurch station. The sale, conducted in April, attracted a large number of gentlemen who arrived by train from London. Prices ranged from £16 to £18 per plot for the erection of bungalows and villas. The local paper also commented upon a rumour that land had also been sold at Eastchurch by a Sittingbourne firm for the purpose of establishing a jam factory.

On the 17th April work began in earnest upon building the tramway when men arrived to break up the roadway on Klondyke Hill. The news of the electric tramway and the increasing traffic being carried on the light railway was duly reported and apparently read far and wide since there was an interest in Sheppey as never before. A month later Mr Ramuz organised another of his popular sales, but this time on the Brambledown Estate. The morning was described as being delightfully bright and breezy as visitors travelled down from London, changing at Queenborough onto the train waiting in the bay platform. It was said the groups 'enjoyed a rural walk and sat down to a feast'. This was held in a marquee where Sheppey mutton was served to those who had worked up an appetite in the fresh, clean air. Many plots were disposed of during the day's business, including a corner site adjacent to the railway station which, it emerged, was intended for a hotel.

Whereas on one hand there appeared to be so many improvements being made in Sheppey, the SE & CR was frequently the butt of criticism over its attitude towards the island. From newspaper reports it seems that the trains very rarely ran to time, connections between the light railway and the main system at Queenborough were often missed, but it was the withdrawal of cheap fares from the 8.45am train which caused the greatest indignation:

> 'For the past eighteen years – in fact ever since Sir Edward Watkin brought the blessing of railway competition to Sheerness by opening up the Port Victoria route, cheap return tickets to London have been issued by the second or thereabouts morning train from Sheerness – that leaving at 8.45am. Although the amalgamation of the two companies has resulted in the removal of competition and the closing of the Port Victoria route, the town of Sheerness cannot, we believe, be deprived of its cheap trains without the sanction of the Board of Trade. The SE & CR have ceased issuing cheap tickets for the 8.45am train, instead they insist passengers travel by the 10.40am which is too late and has a journey time to the metropolis of nearly three hours. It seems that Sheppey is at the tender mercies of railway monopoly.'

As spring turned to summer so the great national event of 1902 was celebrated locally – the coronation of King Edward VII. The original festivities had to be postponed due to the monarch's ill health, but a few weeks later a great day was enjoyed by all. The village of Eastchurch was gaily decorated and stretched across the roadway next to the station was a large banner reading 'WELCOME'. Thoughtfully, a special invitation was sent to the dejected inhabitants of Elmley, requesting them to come and join in the festivities. Messrs Higgs, the chief

---

FREEHOLD LAND.

125,000 Plots for Sale.

EASY PAYMENTS and ..
IMMEDIATE POSSESSION.

Near Sheerness East—Main Road, Halfway Houses to the Abbey, Minster East Station, from **£30** each.

Brambledown, Minster, from **£15** each.

Eastchurch Station, fr
Tilbury Docks Station
Westcliff-on-Sea, fro
Herne Bay, West Cli
Walton-on-Naze, fro
Pitsea Junction, from
Minton-on-Sea Cliffs
Minster Cliffs, Sera
Rochford Town Esta
Rayleigh Station, fi

Scrap's Gate, M
Comfortable Freel
without Land.
ABBEY, MINSTER.
adjoining Minster
UPPER WARDS and
Land and Orchar
LOWER WARDS and
Residence and Fi
BONSTAL HALL, M
and Extensive B
site on the Islan
TADWELL FARMHO
Homestead, ad
Railway Siding
CHEQUER'S LODG
Brick and Sla
Choice Grounds
SPRING LODGE, M
Good Land, O
Land.
Also LAND near
per Plot.
Also SWANLEY
Buildings. T
Price, **£100**
SIMPSON HALL
£600.
TAM'S FARM an
tered, choices
Pair of Main R
near Minster

We are opei
each case. M
Any size to sui
Fare li

Free Con
Ten per c

Apply ..
TH
67 and 6

SHORE

MINSTER-ON-SEA,

Adjacent to the New East Minster Railway Station in close proximity to Minster Village and the Coastguard Station, at Scrap's Gate; within a few minutes of the Halfway Houses, abutting, and have frontage, of valuable character for building upon the Main Road from Sheerness and Queenborough, to Minster.

THE REMAINING 125 ELIGIBLE PLOTS
OF
FREEHOLD BUILDING LAND,

Conveniently Situate on the **Station Estate,** where building operations are already in progress.

Facing Sheerness Road, Sunnyside and Seaville Avenues, and Silverdale Drive. Eminently adapted for the erection of Villas, Cottages, and Bungalows.

MR. GEO. RAMUZ

WILL SELL the above by Auction, in a Marquee on the Estate on

WEDNESDAY, August 20th,
At 2 o'clock p.m.

Luncheon will be provided for intending purchasers at One o'clock.

Payment may be made by Easy Instalments.

FREE DEEDS. ROADS MADE FREE.

Sale Particulars obtainable at all Local Hotels and Inns, and of the Auctioneer, or—

THE LAND COMPANY,
68, CHEAPSIDE, E.C.

IMPORTANT NOTICE.

To the Inhabitants of Sheerness and Queenborough, and the Isle of Sheppey.

The NEW ESTATE OFFICE,

Recently erected for us,

Adjoining EAST MINSTER STATION,

IS NOW OPEN, and is under the management of Mr. Louis Ramuz, who will be pleased to meet intending purchasers, and to give all necessary information concerning our

ORIGINAL EASY PAYMENT SYSTEM

And particulars of Plots for Sale.

The LAND COMPANY,
68, CHEAPSIDE, E.C.

landowners in Warden, had business interests in London, so arrangements were made for their employees and their families to spend the day on the island. The mid-morning train duly steamed into Eastchurch station packed with the happy, excited band who spilled out of the carriages even before the train had come to a complete standstill. At Warden Court a substantial meat dinner and tea was put on for the guests where large makeshift tables were erected in a barn. Numerous entertainments delighted everyone. These included races for the boys and girls, egg-and-spoon, tug-of-war, Aunt Sally and finally a baby contest for the proud mums. Crowding onto the 7.03pm from Eastchurch station, the excitement of a two-hour train journey back home rounded off a memorable day for those children who had probably never been further from their homes than their legs could carry them.

As well as the seasonal opening of the light railway to Leysdown, a further train was introduced in July. This left Queenborough at 2.20pm and returned from Leysdown at 3.10pm. It was a distinctly leisurely ride with forty minutes allowed from start to finish, but at least there was plenty of time to take in the scenery. While this addition was no doubt appreciated, great inconvenience and annoyance was caused in the following month:

> 'The SE & CR do not care one iota how they inconvenience the general public and waste their time. This is how they deal with passengers by the Light Railway. Last Monday, being Bank Holiday, they elected to alter the times of their trains for that day and for the day previous. On Sunday the first morning train was taken off and another run about an hour or so later, so that a number of persons from Upper Sheppey failed to make the connection with the first Sunday train from Queenborough, and consequently had to wait at Queenborough or elsewhere till the afternoon, before they could proceed on their journey. On Monday a service different from the usual weekday service was run, causing much annoyance and inconvenience. Probably the manager, with the best of intentions, has an idea that such alterations of departure &c are for the benefit of the public, but what shall be said of the blundering capacity of officials who alter train services and have special time bills printed for the same and then send them to various stations after the event! Yet such was actually the case, for the timetables for Sunday and Monday were not received at the Light Railway Stations until about the middle of Monday afternoon. Such disregard of the public convenience and blundering stupidity cannot be too strongly denounced.'

In spite of this upset, the Bank Holiday was generally a success for the railway and the traders of Sheerness who looked forward to these opportunities to augment their annual takings. Although the weather proved to be typically English and remained distinctly unsettled, the visitors stoically braved the sporadic showers which threatened to ruin the precious holiday. The SE & CR found their trains well-patronised 'with barely a seat to spare', whilst great excitement was caused on Monday when at noon the crowds thronged onto the promenade to witness the mighty four-funnelled cruiser *Bacchante* steam into the docks.

The light railway had now been operating for just over a year and it would be an accurate assumption to say that it had exceeded most people's expectations. Receipts were healthy and it had proved every bit as popular as had been so confidently predicted by its promoters – a rare occurrence indeed. It was unquestionably a great boon to the farmers and tradesmen along the route. However, it seems it was a victim of its own success for complaints began to land on the SE & CR's desk of insufficient facilities being offered at the sidings and stations.

Although William Rigby had since relinquished all control and responsibility, there were still matters which demanded attention and these would have to be remedied by the SE & CR. Of particular concern was the poor state of the many level crossings along the line where the road surface had broken up. Landowners were equally perturbed by 'inadequate' fencing which often led to livestock wandering onto the track and delaying the trains.

At the end of October the Eastchurch–Leysdown section was once again closed to passengers for five months until 1st April, while the winter timetable reverted to four weekday trains each way and two on Sunday. In the meantime, the council were still at battle with the SE & CR over the 'cheap' 8.45am train to London. It transpired that far from considering its reintroduction, the SE & CR were planning to reduce the number of cheap tickets still further.

With the Sheerness tramway rapidly taking shape and the new light railway operating successfully, attention was drawn to the poor state of the island's roads which had been largely neglected. Mr Kite, a road-building contractor, complained to the council that supplies of flint and ragstone were not coming in fast enough to keep his men fully employed. Nor was there enough daily work for his team of horses in transporting the materials from the light railway to the sites and on one occasion they'd remained in their stables for four days. Although some of the blame was laid on the sharp frosts of January 1903, the main cause rested with insufficient room at Harty siding, where just two trucks could be left. Therefore, Mr Kite asked the council to see if extra truckloads could be delivered to Eastchurch. This arrangement appears to have been satisfactory.

During January the SE & CR sought permission to dispense with the gates at Harty Road level crossing. Since they had already been run through on one occasion, it was suggested that cattle guards be substituted. Councillor Till strongly opposed the idea, since he thought the gradient too steep at that point and without gates the trains might be tempted to go faster whereby any deaf person or child might be knocked down. He added that there was no station for almost two miles in either direction, nor was there a man employed there to warn people when the train was approaching. Councillor Dickson thought the motive behind the request was that the SE & CR didn't want the bother of stopping the trains there since it fell to the train's guard to open and shut the gates. As a result, the application was refused.

Other railway developments were also taking place during this time. The SE & CR were busy extending their line into the dockyard, whilst across the Medway the Port Victoria service was reinstated on 14th April. Concerning the latter, the *Sheerness Times* commented somewhat tersely: 'There is a service of eight trains daily, but in the absence of any boat connection, the line is valueless so far as Sheerness is concerned'.

On Thursday, 9th April 1903, the tramway opened to the public with great success, many Sheerness people using it over the following weekend to reach Sheerness East station where they boarded trains for Leysdown. The *Sheerness Times* commented upon the recent developments:

> 'We have this week to congratulate the Electric Tramway Company upon the inauguration of the tram service between Sheerness East and Cheyney Rock. We wish the venture every success and trust that it may prove beneficial to the town, and profitable to the Company, whose enterprise has brought into our midst this adjunct of advanced civilization. The Isle of Sheppey with its light railway, and electric trams has made great strides within the last few years. . . .'

A rather serious accident involving the light railway took place later that month, on the afternoon of Thursday, 23rd April.

A tram bound for Sheerness East, swaying along the track through the Broadway on a sunny summer's afternoon. The elegant design of the overhead feeders is clearly seen, as is the unusual (unique to Britain) Siemens bow current collectors. *Collection Richard Cullen*

Around two o'clock a motor car with military officers was speeding towards Sheerness East station on its way to Eastchurch. On nearing the level crossing, which at that time had its gates closed to the road, the driver mistook the entrance to the tramway shed for the main road. At the last moment a voice shouted 'No, go to the right', whereupon the driver swerved and promptly knocked over Mr Thomas, the station master, who was waiting to close the gates behind the approaching train. The poor man disappeared beneath the car as it smashed through one gate before stopping across the railway track. Prompt action by the engine driver brought the train to a shuddering halt, barely inches from crushing the car and its passengers. The station master was taken to the local hospital in a serious condition with a bad wound to the back of his head. Fortunately he regained consciousness in the evening and eventually recovered. The local paper praised the engine driver for preventing the car's occupants from going underneath his train, adding: 'It is no wonder that motor cars get into disrepute with those who do not use them, for as a rule they are driven at too high a speed for the safety of the public, and if a gate across a roadway cannot be seen in time to pull up, how is the solitary pedestrian likely to fare?'

The summer of 1903 proved to be most prosperous for both the light railway and the tramway. At Whitsun the trams were crowded with standing room only between the Clock Tower and Sheerness East. Here, people alighted in droves to board the trains for Leysdown which, in spite of sparse facilities, retained its popularity. On Whitsun Monday alone over 1,350 passengers were carried on the light railway as every seat was reported to have been occupied.

The grand coronation clock tower in Sheerness which exemplified civic pride and became a popular meeting place.

Author's collection

While the trams did their best to complement the light railway service, there were, however, complaints to the company that the 2.11pm train from Sheerness East to Leysdown was often missed which 'made access to the more rural localities difficult'. There was also much discontent over the rates being charged by the SE & CR, while it was claimed that English farmers nationally were at a distinct disadvantage when competing with their foreign counterparts. Mr Boorman of Old Hook Farm was upset at being charged three shillings at Minster station to send eight fowls to Sheerness, a distance of four miles. He argued 'It is only fourpence less than a party of eight people for the same journey!' The local paper sympathised: 'The Light Railway was heralded as a great boon to the farmers and stockowners of Sheppey, but if this is a sample of the charges then the time has surely arrived when an attempt should be made to secure a reduced tariff.'

Whilst there would always be some who were dissatisfied with the rates and service being offered by the SE & CR on the Sheppey Light, others considered the line a most useful addition to the system. In a rather charming little piece contributed by 'Idler', a trip along the line was summed up thus:

'OUR LIGHT RAILWAY:
From Whitstable I travelled to Sittingbourne, so called because you have to sit for so long on the platform to wait for a train. Ultimately I reached Queenborough on the Isle of Sheppey. Now, Sheppey is interesting from the fact that a new light railway has been built there, clear across the island from the West to the East Coast, for nine tempestuous miles, over hill and down dale. Yet the little train is of the most modern description, being vestibuled and corridored, just as if it were the "edition de luxe" running to Nice. A friendly guard comes through and charges you ninepence for a ticket which takes you the length of the line. He furnishes the ticket, punches a hole in the ninepenny part, and then sits down and chats with you, telling you who owns the farms on each side of the railway. I wanted to keep the ticket, for it is a most entertaining bit of literature, about six inches by four inches, rectangular, containing much useful information regarding the rules under which the Light Railway works. But the guard gently detached it from me at the end of the line, because he has to keep a check on himself to see that he returns the right amount of money to the company. He was a most useful and energetic man: when we came to a crossing the train stopped,

This trackside view of the Leysdown terminus illustrates the livestock pens, part of the goods yard and the operational details of the starting signal.
Collection Reg Randell

Leysdown station about 1904, showing the original SLR fencing and platform facing. The SE & CR's eventual improvements removed something of the line's rustic character.
Lens of Sutton

Kitson & Co.'s steam railmotor No. 1 on the Leysdown service at Queenborough in 1905. The trailer car attached to the unit bore the legend 'Sheppey Light Railway' above the centre compartment window.
Dr. Evers courtesy R. L. Ratcliffe

he got out and opened the two gates, then the train pulled through and he closed the two gates, coming after us in a gentle trot.'

Despite the grumbling from local farmers over the railway rates, its usefulness was undeniable. At Christmas the market ground next to Eastchurch station was thronged with dealers and animals for the Annual Fat Stock Show. These events were due solely to the railway, as were the dreams of developing Sheppey.

At the first annual dinner of the high-sounding 'Leysdown and Shellness-on-Sea Building Estate Company', held at the Holborn Restaurant in London, a hundred guests sat down to hear the latest aspirations. Plans for a golf course and motor racing track were revealed, whilst the needs of yachtsmen were soon promised attention. Perhaps the most ambitious hope came in reference to the railway to Leysdown when it was claimed: 'The estate will rival Brighton and Southend for with the railway communications it is possible to leave London and reach Leysdown in less than two hours'. However, the fact that both Brighton and Southend could be reached far more quickly and directly seems to have been conveniently overlooked.

During 1904 the *Sheerness Times* announced that the SE & CR would be applying to parliament for powers to purchase the Sheppey Light Railway: 'we take it from their action that the line is proving a success and hope it will continue to prosper'. The purchase of the line had, in fact, been the intention almost from the start since in August 1902 an agreement was reached that it would exchange hands for £65,000.

As a result of the complaints over the inadequacy of the sidings at Harty Road and Brambledown crossings, the SE & CR extended these during 1903. Further improvements were to follow at the stations where concrete facings to the platforms replaced the redundant sleepers, whilst iron railings did away with the rotting trellis fencing. Fluted iron lamp posts were also erected.

Around this time the SE & CR was obliged to look for more economical means of operating its branch lines and lesser-used routes. During 1904 Sir Edward Leigh-Pemberton, chairman of the LC & DR*, revealed that there had been an alarming decrease in the number of passengers over that year – down by 2,178,475.

The editorial in the *Sheerness Times* considered the reason was:

'....undoubtedly the competition created by the establishment of tramways in the suburbs of London. These are being found to be more convenient and cheaper and in some cases faster than railway travelling, to say nothing of the advantages of comfort which the trams confer compared with stuffy railway carriages'.

Rather than curtail services, it was decided that railcars, or railmotors as they were sometimes known, should be given trials. In his book *Locomotives of the South Eastern and Chatham Railway*, Don Bradley gives an interesting account of how this came about. Preliminary runs were made on the Sheppey Light during late September 1903 with two small petrol-electric railcars which were borrowed from Dick, Kerr & Co. They were not very successful though, especially on frosty mornings when the familiar ignition problems with internal combustion engines were experienced. Hot water for the radiators had to be obtained from standby steam locomotives, whilst obligatory push-starts must have amused engine crews who likely scoffed at this infant technology. One of the railcars could carry only four passengers, so it was clearly quite useless, but the other had seating for eighteen. Bradley comments that had the SE & CR been able to have found a qualified motor mechanic then this railcar would have been purchased, but such men were rare in 1903. Of the two applicants for the job, one refused to move from Chatham to Sheerness, whilst the other demanded a higher wage than that paid to locomotive fitters. As a result, it was eventually decided by H. S. Wainwright, the SE & CR's locomotive superintendent, that orders should be placed with Messrs Kitson & Co. Ltd of the Airdale Foundry in Leeds for two steam driven railmotors.

---

*Although working together as one organization, the LC & DR and SER remained separate companies.

Left: Railmotor No. 1 in the platform at Leysdown during the summer of 1905, with SE & CR No. 751 on the loop road with the Sheppey goods brake. *Below:* The ex-LB & SCR 'Terrier' class locomotive, formerly *Waddon*, purchased by the SE & CR and nicknamed 'Little Tich' by the crews.
The Railway Magazine and collection Peter Harding

Following trials between Dover and Deal, as well as Ashford and New Romney, railcar No. 1 was sent to Sheerness for the Leysdown services. In February 1905 the *Sheerness Times* reported:

> 'QUEENBOROUGH: – STEAM MOTOR CAR:
> On Tuesday [14th] the ordinary train was withdrawn from the Sheppey Light Railway and replaced by a steam motor car, which is 56 ft in length and is capable of travelling at a speed of 30 miles an hour. The car, which is very comfortable has accommodation for fifty passengers and another fifty can be accommodated in the trailer, which will be stored at Queenborough and will only be used when required. The motor was constructed [partly] at Ashford and Mr Thompson, the superintendent of the line, travelled in it on Monday on the trial run from Ashford to Leysdown. First class fares on the Light Railway are now abolished, only third class tickets being issued.'

Seating was divided into non-smoking (32) and smoking (24) compartments, with electric lighting. The new unit was finished in the smart crimson lake livery of the SE & CR and even had 'SHEPPEY LIGHT RAILWAY' specially signwritten on the sides. Since the reason behind their introduction had been one of economy, the SE & CR carried out an experiment specifically to ascertain what comparisons might be made. Accordingly, a log was kept of engine No. 523 and a train of three six-wheel carriages on a trip to Leysdown and back, as well as the same run using the railcar. The result spoke for itself:

	Cost per mile	*Coal burnt per mile*
No.523 & train	£2 1s 6d	26¾ lbs
Railcar	£1 5s 0d	15¼ lbs

Following the introduction of the railcar, the SE & CR speeded up the service, the run between Queenborough and Leysdown being completed in half an hour, an improvement of ten minutes. However, this had more to do with a lax timetable, rather than the railcars being faster or more powerful. In fact, quite the reverse was true, but the Sheppey railway never seems to have caused them the problems of lack of tractive effort which they experienced on other routes.

The winter of 1904–5 saw some extraordinary high tides, as well as a 'tidal wave' which caused damage around the island and other parts of North Kent. The weather soon settled into spring, however, as minds turned to the approaching season. In March an application was made for a hotel licence at Leysdown because, it was claimed, with the establishment of a golf links,

there was nowhere for Londoners to stay. The proposed grand structure, costing £6,000, was surprisingly turned down, leaving visitors to make do with the rather limited overnight accommodation on offer at the local inn.

Not everyone welcomed the changes taking place on the island and in the wayside villages along the way. A correspondent, signing him or herself 'Visitor' wrote of the surprising trip:

> 'Instead of the old-time butcher's shop there is now a new confectionery establishment where, I suppose, the temporary visitor will be able to get the stereotyped cup of tea, roll and butter.'

As for the Light Railway:

> 'This ought to be a benefit to the village proper, but the trains ought to run more frequently, as I found the times very inconvenient. However, I suppose this will come in time.'

The freight business remained steadfast, but following the withdrawal of ordinary trains and the mixed services, there was, of course, a need to run special goods trains. On 5th July 1904 the SE & CR had written to its neighbouring company, the London, Brighton and South Coast Railway, enquiring whether they had any spare locomotives for purchase which would be suitable for working the Sheppey Light. The LB & SCR came up with an 0–6–0 tank engine, No.54, originally named *Waddon*, which was eventually handed over in August at Hastings for £670. Renumbered 751 by the SE & CR, the locomotive was sent to the island and began working the freight on 12th February 1905. It soon established itself as a useful and popular engine with the crews, indeed it was taken to their hearts so much that its diminutive form earned it the nickname of *Little Tich* after Harry Relph, a well-known contemporary music hall performer.

The 'Sheppey Goods' was not an arduous task for 751. A start was made from Queenborough at ten to four in the afternoon where it ran to Leysdown calling all stations, except East Minster-on-Sea, to arrive at ten past five. For twenty minutes the yard was shunted before departure at 5.32 and arrival back at Queenborough fifty-five minutes later. When not working the goods, or occasionally substituting for the railcar, No.751 went off to potter about on shunting duties in the dockyard.

Coinciding with the introduction of the railcars, the SE & CR opened two new stops along the line for the convenience of the locals. Harty Road Halt, between Leysdown and Eastchurch, and Brambledown Halt, between Eastchurch and Minster, were brought into use in March. During that month the SE & CR again approached the District Council with a view to substituting cattle guards for the crossing gates 'now that the railcars are running'. There was little sympathy, the chairman remarking it was 'funny for the company to ask a favour of the council when they have never complied with the council's requests' [they were still seeking the reinstatement of the 8.45am 'cheap' train]. They considered that sanitary accommodation should be provided at all the stations, while councillor Dickson wanted to know why 'anyone getting into a train at Brambledown Siding was charged the same fare as passengers from Minster'. Councillor Castle added: 'The same fare is charged from Harty Siding to Eastchurch as from Leysdown'. The council therefore refused 'until fares were reduced and lavatories were provided'. The local paper took up the issue, commenting 'amalgamation has proved a gigantic disappointment and there will be no prospect of improvement until there is competition to break the current monopoly'. In somewhat bitter terms it continued:

'The Rural District Council is to be commended upon the firmness displayed with regard to the application from the SE & CR Company to substitute cattle guards instead of gates at various points where the Sheppey Light Railway crosses the highways. For a long time past the council has been unavailingly calling upon the Company to provide proper sanitary arrangements at the various stations on the light railway, but so far their representations have passed unheeded. For the sake of those who use the line, to say nothing of public decency, we certainly expected more consideration would be shown by the Company and until they listen to the representations of the Council and take some steps to remedy the grievances complained of, the Council will be quite justified in refusing to make any further concession to the Company. From the inauguration of the Light Railway until the present time, every consideration has been shown to the proprietors of the line, and in their desire to see the rural portion of Sheppey opened up to railway communication there can be no doubt that the Council executed many public works in the way of widening and making up the approaches to the stations, that the company might reasonably have been expected to carry out, and the turning of a deaf ear to their repeated request for the provision of adequate conveniences at stations is a poor return for all the concessions made and the favours shown the promoters.'

A further sale of freehold building land took place on 5th July, but this time at Leysdown where intentions of creating a new seaside resort were still being expressed. An encouraging number of prospective purchasers arrived on the morning train, eager to inspect the numerous plots which were marked up for sale. Midday luncheon at 'The Rose & Crown' sustained the buyers before the afternoon's business commenced. Returning by train and tram to 'The Britannia Hotel' at Sheerness, about seventy gentlemen sat down to a hearty dinner before hearing Mr J. Tower speak of the attractions of the location where they purchased land that day. He pointed out that the estate was only fifty miles from London Bridge, while the terminus of the Sheppey Light Railway was situated on part of that estate, being only a few yards from the sea. Leysdown, he claimed, could boast of having about 1,000 acres of prime land fit for development, together with a sea frontage of nearly three miles. He concluded: 'The SE & CR is moving with the times and you will know by your journey today that the electric* motor on the Light Railway conveyed you in half the time that the locomotive service could accomplish the distance. There is no doubt that as the place grows in size, the journey from London will be covered in less than an hour and a half.'

The Isle of Sheppey throughout the summer months was undeniably a pleasant spot, especially Leysdown in the rural eastern corner, away from the noisome and rather offensive industries gathered around the western side. It is hardly surprising, therefore, that with the new modes of transport the residents of Queenborough and Sheerness took the opportunity at weekends for a breath of fresh air and a paddle. One particularly enjoyable occasion was the annual outing of the wives and children of the Royal Naval Gunnery School at Sheerness. Customarily the event was held in the meadow adjoining the school, but in 1905 it was decided to be more venturesome and visit Leysdown. Gathering at the Clock Tower, around 170 children were escorted onto the waiting trams for a speedy ride to Sheerness East station. Here they boarded the railmotor, which had the trailer car attached, whereupon they arrived at Leysdown at a quarter past one. The children were soon running off down Station Road to the beach and enjoying themselves at the water's edge. Sports and games were arranged during the afternoon, with a break for tea at four o'clock. The weather was 'all that could be desired' and it seems that everyone was reluctant to leave the beach at seven o'clock for the sunshine was still warm on this balmy evening. At Leysdown station they again piled into the railcar, no doubt fighting for a window seat, before an exciting ride once more across the fields and meadows to Sheerness East. After a quick ride by tram, the happy band reached the clock tower at 8.30pm, tired and weary but 'thoroughly satisfied and delighted with the day's outing'.

Whereas the railcars initially promised to be the answer to the SE & CR's financial problems, they were neither popular with engine crews nor the public who were accustomed to the conventional trains. Drivers apparently resented being allocated these rosters, complaining that the footplate was cramped, very hot and uncomfortable. The ride was often very rough, particularly with the engine pushing from the rear, and oscillation throughout the whole unit eventually necessitated modifications a couple of years later. An interesting account of a ride in a railmotor appeared in print in July 1905:

'Sir – When I took a ticket the other day at Sheerness East for a run through the 'Unknown Paradise' I certainly had more than I bargained for. I had an impression that the motor train would be at least as 'luxurious' as the SE & CR thirds usually are; but before almost I had time to take stock of surroundings it was bump, bump, bang, bang, bang. Every stroke of the piston was a jar that made one wish the journey was at an end. I got further and further away from the engine – the apparent cause of the commotion, but it made little difference, – bump, bump, bang, bang, was still the order of going. To put such a jolty contrivance upon rails for carrying passengers reflects highly upon the capacity, cleverness and ingenuity of the Company. Why, it is as bad as going over the headers that used to pave the High Street of Blue Town in a heavy cart without springs. This is progression of the twentieth century with a vengeance.

'Another most admirable arrangement is that no windows are made to open – a veritable oven, a regular cooking stove for poor humanity. When will the SE & CR come to recognise the wants of the public, and the duty of the company to meet them?
Yours etc,
'BONE-SHAKEN'

---

*The motor was, of course, steam not electric.

Far from heeding such criticism, the SE & CR decided to order further units as revealed by the *Sheerness Times* on Saturday, 9th September:

> 'MOTOR TRAINS:
> The experimental motor train service tried by the SE & C Railway on the Sheppey Branch has proved so successful that it has been decided to place them on other branches and six new trains are being constructed for this purpose at their Ashford works.

The curious-looking Hungarian-built railcar which is said to have spent a short time on trials over the Sheppey Light during October 1905.
Collection Dave Gilbert

> 'This paragraph is copied from "The Times" but we doubt whether those who travel by the motor service between Queenborough and Leysdown will agree with the writer as to the success of the motor train service.'

A few weeks later it was reported that railcar No.1 had been sent off from Queenborough to Ashford 'for inspection'. Great relief seems to have greeted the return of *Little Tich* and its set of five aged, but comfortable, six-wheeled carriages. However, it wasn't long before the railmotor returned, only to disappear once again to Ashford as revealed by the local paper:

> 'The Light Railway "bumper" which attained such notoriety during the summer months was sent to hospital at Ashford to cure it of its pranks, returned to its duties in Sheppey about a fortnight since, but in consequence of a rapid renewal of its incongruities had to be again dispatched to hospital for a trial of indoor cure.'

By now the islanders were probably well-accustomed to the antics of their light railway 'bumper', but it seemed the SE & CR was determined to introduce railcars in some form or another to save costs. There can only have been a mixture of consternation and disbelief, therefore, when a few months later, in October 1905, a most peculiar contraption was sent down for trials. This was the 'Peebles' steam rail car built by Ganz & Co. of Budapest for use on the Hungarian railways. It was initially tested on the Midland Railway between Loughborough and Derby before being sent south, presumably being passed around the companies to ascertain whether it might prove useful. It is recorded as having run over the Westerham branch on the 12th and 13th August 1905, before spending five days, between 10th and 15th September trundling along the Medway valley between Paddock Wood and Maidstone. At some time it is believed to have also been tried out on the L & SWR's Basingstoke-Alton line. However, it was evidently of little use to the SE & CR and it was mercifully decided not to permanently inflict this even more uncomfortable-looking hybrid on the islanders.

In spite of these trials and tribulations with the light railway trains, the traffic on both the Leysdown branch and the Sheerness tramway was very healthy, with some days proving quite hectic. Such a day was that in late August when a land sale at Minster attracted hundreds of buyers. Having arrived at Sheerness pier from London by one of the Belle Company's steamers, six trams had to be specially requisitioned to transport the party to Sheerness East station. However, the generating station was quite unable to cope with the load, whereupon the line of trams came to a halt on the Halfway House Road, leaving the occupants with no choice but to walk the rest of the way. Following this incident the tramway company installed new feeders from Sheerness East to the Queen's Head.

Three years after the opening of the railway, it became apparent that something would need to be done to remedy the lack of water at Leysdown for the locomotives. Authorisation to drill for a supply had been given in July 1904, while a contract worth £625 was entered into with J. Warner & Son to erect a windmill with pumping apparatus and pipes. A rather amusing although unsubstantiated tale exists that while drilling the borehole the bit came across a stratum of hard rock, which diverted it sideways. Drilling continued since all appeared to be going to plan, but it was only when the cutting head of the bit suddenly re-emerged through the surface some feet away that the workmen realised what had happened. The fact that excess expenditure of £330 was granted in July 1905 and the final bill in 1906 amounted to £1,295, double the estimate, does at least give some credence to this story.

There were most likely groans of disapproval on the morning of 19th May 1906 when the normal train on the light railway was replaced by a railmotor which came wheezing along the line. This time, railcar No.6 was used since No.1 was still having its boiler and firebox attended to at Ashford railway works. In the event, No.6 remained at Sheerness, whilst No.1 eventually went off to infuriate the regular travellers on the Westerham

The approach to Minster from the foot of the hill, approximately at the point where the extension of the Sheerness tramway was to have terminated. Windmill Cottages, on the right, have long since disappeared, but Prospect Villa behind the trees still stands. Behind this house is a steep alleyway, leading up to the Gate House and church, and charmingly known as Dancing Dolly Hill.

Collection Martin Hawkins

branch in West Kent. As for the ex-LC & DR locomotives, it is almost certain that Nos. 518, 520 and 523, were still in charge of the Leysdown services.

All three were reboilered during 1906-7 but their active days were numbered and they spent their twilight years pottering around the island. No.518 was the first to go, withdrawn in July 1909 and scrapped at Longhedge where its boiler was salvaged and sent to Ashford to be converted for laundry work, lasting until 1934. No.520 was withdrawn in August, its number being transferred to one of the new 'H' class locomotives currently nearing completion at Ashford. Finally, No.523 was taken out of service in September.

A rather congenial occasion was the annual dinner for the Sheppey Light Railway employees, an unusual custom which continued for many years in spite of the fact that the branch had been wholly absorbed into the SE & CR. It would seem that the men were proud of their little line and determined to hold onto its identity. At the Public Hall in Minster on the evening of Saturday, 7th December 1907, glasses were raised to the customary toast – 'Success to the Sheppey Light Railway!'. The chairman, Mr H. C. Warren told the gathering that the line had proved to be 'a perfect Godsend to the farmers'. Elaborating, he spoke of the healthy level of trade now being carried both ways on the branch, the benefits it had brought to the farming community and villagers and how the future prospects of the isle were so rosy. He had praise, too, for the men gathered there and he thought the light railway staff were especially obliging: 'When standing on a platform it has sometimes puzzled me how many and varied are the questions put to the staff – and yet they always manage to keep on giving civil answers' [laughter].

In spite of the fact that the Sheppey Light has lost its independent status and was now a mere branch of the 'great railway', it retained its backwater atmosphere throughout its existence. The staff employed at the stations were part of the community, whilst there was always a cheery wave from the locomotive crews to the local children who sat upon the wayside stiles. Life without the railway had become almost unthinkable since it had more than proved its worth to the farmers, landowners, villagers and annual visitors.

Around this time, plans were revealed to build the world's longest pier at Minster-on-Sea and the scheme even went so far as to gain the approval of the Board of Trade. Extending 7,000 feet into the sea, the mammoth structure was designed to outmatch the one boasted by Southend. To complement this anticipated attraction and the hopeful development of Minster, an application was made to the Light Railway Commissioners by Mr George Ramuz and others for an extension of the tramway from Sheerness East to Minster.

At a length of 1 mile 24 chains, and costing an estimated £4,970, the 3 ft 6 in gauge line was planned to be an extension of the Sheerness & District Company's system. Commencing at a junction immediately behind Sheerness East station, where the original tramway curved sharply into the depot, the Minster route aimed to run parallel with the railway as far as Drove Road. From here it swung north, almost at a right-angle, before curving eastwards once again to cross Kent Avenue. Passing over The Broadway and Waverley Avenue, it accompanied

Woodland Drive, then crossed over Glenwood Drive and Wybornes Chase, before terminating at the foot of Minster Hill. The proposed extension traversed fairly hilly country, with varying gradients, the steepest being 1 in 14.

Not surprisingly, the 'Minster-on-Sea Light Railway' was vigorously opposed by the SE & CR, who insisted it would detract business from the Leysdown branch. It is also apparent that they suspected its eventual success would lead to further proposals to extend beyond to Eastchurch and, perhaps, Leysdown. Fortunately for the SE & CR, other objectors, mostly small private landowners, added their voices against the scheme, which soon led to its downfall. Nevertheless, it was hardly a victory for the ordinary islanders and folk of Minster who would, undoubtedly, have benefited from this convenient and easily accessible system of transport.

The proposal to extend the tramway to Minster was not only in response to the desire to develop Minster-on-Sea, but also the reputedly poor service offered by the SE & CR. George Ramuz complained bitterly to the council, stating that repeated applications for a more satisfactory service had been ignored. Mr Charles Ingleton, JP, of Borstal Hall added his support, commenting that there was scarcely sufficient time to travel from Eastchurch station to London and back to allow a day's business transactions. He claimed the service was so inconvenient that he often took to driving his trap to Queenborough in order that he might reach his home later that evening. Others agreed, whilst councillor Warren asked if first class accommodation might be restored, but the clerk simply 'wished the line was more patronised'.

Later that same year Minster Parish Council complained to the SE & CR about the level crossing at Minster-on-Sea station. Here, the gates closed on one side only, in their view constituting a great danger since 'visitors had actually been on the line when the train was approaching'. Miraculously, no one ever appears to have been knocked down here or at any of the eleven level crossings between Queenborough and Leysdown. However, there were occasional incidents which sometimes made the local press, one such item appearing in August 1909:

> 'Just after noon on Tuesday, a man employed by Mr T. H. Curtis was engaged in loading a van with sacks of coal at the Sheerness East railway siding. The horse was standing quietly in the shafts when the headpiece of the harness (which includes the blinkers) slipped, thus giving the horse a full view. The horse at once bolted. Coming to the fence which separates the railway siding from the roadway, the animal leapt clean over and the front wheels of the van caught the stout wooden fence which it broke like matchwood. By this time the man had jumped from the cart, without injury. The horse safely dashed past a couple of tramcars on the Halfway House Road before coming to the Crescent where it slipped and fell. Fortunately no damage occurred to horse or vehicle.'

Whereas Leysdown's development was disappointingly proving to be far slower than had been originally anticipated, it was the turn of another part of the isle to gain notoriety. Early in the spring of 1909 the Aero Club of Great Britain, reputedly the leading authority on aviation, was looking for a suitable site to create an aerodrome for the emerging technology. It is not known who suggested the Isle of Sheppey to the famous Wright brothers, but during that season both Orville and Wilbur Wright travelled down to Eastchurch. Wilbur Wright was overawed by what he found; 'The most beautiful grounds for flying' he exclaimed, 'The best and most ideal I have ever seen'. The Stone Pits Marshes were chosen for an auxiliary flying ground, while workshops and other facilities were quickly established. In the following year, 1910, it was reported that the flat marshes at Leysdown and Shellness were to be designated proper flying grounds and the news of this created much interest both locally and nationally. As a result, the Easter holiday saw well over a thousand spectators descending on Eastchurch. Most people came down by train, whereby the light railway was crowded all day. Members of the Aero Club and more affluent individuals

A rare glimpse from the platform of East Minster on Sea as SE & CR No. 520, formerly LC & DR *Crampton*, pauses to pick up passengers bound for Queenborough. *Lens of Sutton*

'Wonderful days they were, almost prehistoric in the history of flight, and in the long, long years to come men will come to this place and say, "This is where it happened".' — Arthur Mee. One of many daring aeronautical displays which thrilled the crowds who came to Sheppey to witness the birth of aviation.   *Author's collection*

motored down from London, only to join the charabancs queued up at the King's Ferry toll bridge. Throughout Saturday daring displays and aeronautical tricks astounded and thrilled the spectators. The Hon. C. S. Rolls took a Wright's biplane up into the air and encircled Eastchurch station a number of times.

On Easter Sunday there was even greater interest when a monoplane was shown off for the first time. It was reported that this machine was a Howard-Wright design of the Bleriot type. The Duke of Westminster was present over the holiday and purchased for himself a Voisin biplane. However, the main topic of conversation revolved around the performance by Mr Cecil Grace who took off in his Wright's biplane in order to show it off to the crowds. Unfortunately though, while 'performing certain evolutions in front of the sheds', he lost control of the machine while only thirty feet from the ground and promptly crashed. Miraculously he walked away unscathed, but his pride and joy was reported to be completely wrecked.

The Isle of Sheppey, and Eastchurch in particular, may feel justifiably proud at being so much a part of the history of early aviation in Britain. Sadly, though, neither Cecil Grace nor the Hon. C. S. Rolls lived to see out the year, let alone witness the development of the aeroplane. Rolls died in an aviation accident in the autumn, whilst Grace went missing, presumed drowned, while partaking in the De Forest £4,000 prize competitive flight between Dover and Calais. The *Sheerness Times* mournfully commented: 'Their names will never be forgotten in the Isle of Sheppey'.

In spite of the water pump which the SE & CR had provided some years earlier at Leysdown, it would appear that a shortage was being experienced. This is thought to have been the reason behind the services being taken over by ex-SER Stirling 'O' class 0-6-0 tender engines which had a water capacity of 2,000 gallons – four times that of the little 'Terrier' tank engine No. 751. *Little Tich* therefore left its island home and, following periodic repairs, continued its useful working life for many years. A happy footnote is that in 1963 it was restored to its original 1876 livery before being presented to the Canadian Historical Association and shipped to Montreal later that year.

There was some considerable relief for those who detested being obliged to travel in the 'bone-shaker' when the railcar service was again withdrawn. Some months earlier, unit No. 6 had been replaced by No. 5, but matters didn't improve, so there was probably a feeling of good riddance when it was seen disappearing southwards over the King's Ferry Bridge. The replacement, which came along in September 1910, was one of the new 'P' class 0-6-0T locomotives, fitted for auto-train working and a specially adapted set of ex-LC & DR coaches. With the engine and train being separate, the problems of vibration and rough-riding were obviated, much to the approval of crews and passengers alike. Although the 'P's were the smallest locomotives produced by Harry Wainwright for the SE & CR, they were found to be ideal for such light work as well as shunting duties in various parts of the system.

The last of the really ancient ex-LC & DR locomotives known to have handled the Sheppey services were two members of the 'Large Scotchmen' or Kirtley 'D' class 0-4-2 Well Tanks. Built in 1873, No. 557, originally named *Cambria* and No. 559, *Scotia*, saw out most of their last days here. Notwithstanding their age and condition, Sheerness shed kept them in pristine order and, with their highly-polished paintwork, burnished brasswork and bright red coupling rods, they were a credit to the men. Both engines helped out on the passenger services when the railmotors hadn't been available in the last few years of the Edwardian era. However, their end was near. No. 559 went for scrap in December 1913, whilst No. 557 was at least allowed the dignity of running to Ashford under its own steam for its appointment with the scrapheap in the summer of 1914.

The new auto-trains continued with some success, although the 'P's tractive effort was not all that might be desired. However, the Leysdown trips were usually undemanding and the timings at that period, generally 33 minutes from end to end, were reasonable. The slowness of the journey never seems to have bothered anyone, certainly no evidence of any complaint has been found. Since there were seven stops along the way, no sooner had the regulation 25 mph been reached than it was time to shut off steam and pull up at the next station.

In 1913 approaches were made to the SE & CR to open a halt on the 'main' line at West Minster, between Queenborough and Sheerness. Any advancement of the idea was soon precluded by the outbreak of the Great War and was never resuscitated in the postwar climate of motorised road transport.

During that year the regulars on the light railway were saddened by the death of Frederick Griggs, a 31 year old guard and ticket collector. He was a popular and friendly young man who knew all his local travellers and tradesmen along the line. Born in Deal, he started work as a porter with the LC & DR in 1897 at Westgate-on-Sea, before transferring to Chatham and then to Victoria in 1900. He moved to Queenborough in 1908 where he took up his post on the Leysdown runs. He died as a result of influenza and bronchitis which, in those days, was something to fear. Apart from this occasion, no other deaths connected with the railway have come to light, either during construction or operation, which is surprising. Compared to most other lines, the Sheppey Light was certainly fortunate in this respect.

Each passing season brought changes to the island and the pace of life for those who lived and worked in this detached region of Kent. The mantle of wintertime snow gave way to February's rainsodden fields and bitterly cold winds, before the warming rays of spring sunshine encouraged buds to burst and new shoots to appear. Soon the island was alive once more with the bleating of new-born lambs, the mating songs of birds, as well as the busy humdrum comings and goings of mankind. Summer, with its long, sunny days brought again the day trippers to the 'Unknown Paradise' or 'The Holiday Isle' as it was once popularly termed. Leysdown and Warden Bay slumbered in the quietude that attracted those who sought respite from the hurly-burly of life in the towns and cities. Perhaps it was fortuitous that the widescale development so ardently promoted a decade earlier had failed to appear. Here, there was little but the sound of the gentlest of waves lapping upon a sandy shoreline as the water idly toyed with oddments of jetsam, seaweed and washed-up sea creatures. The outside world was changing fast, although such a notion might well have appeared unbelievable to those in this remote, peaceful place who gazed out across the sweeping marshes to the silvery Swale. Nevertheless, the age of the aeroplane had brought with it apprehensiveness over its capability to rain death and destruction upon civilians. The new

Kirtley 'D' class No. 100 *Scotia* in LC & DR days, renumbered 559 by the SE & CR and used on the Sheppey Light Railway.
Collection John Kite

PALMY DAYS

A Stirling 'O' class starting away from East Minster on Sea with a train for Leysdown in the years immediately preceding the Great War.
Collection Martin Hawkins

dirigibles similarly caused great anxiety, and widespread unease was voiced in the Kentish newspapers when in June 1913 a mighty and mysterious airship had glided silently above Dover. Fear was only heightened a few days later when it was revealed that the strange visitor had been the German Zeppelin, the *Hansa*.

In spite of these worries which troubled most people, there seemed little reason for not making the most of the spells of glorious weather during the summer of 1914. Day trips to the seaside were popular as never before, the trains crowded with people determined to break away from the monotony of work and make the most of the opportunity. Sadly, for so many, it proved to be their last English summer. The Isle of Sheppey remained a firm favourite, not only with those from south London who flocked to Sheerness, but also those who shied away from the brashness of Southend or Brighton, preferring instead the convenient tranquillity of rural Leysdown and Warden. The light railway trains were well-patronised, but equally the roads were busy in a way that had before only rarely been seen. At the beginning of the year motor omnibus services had been established between Sheerness and the villages by private operators. It was stated that no less than seven licences had been applied for by rival organizations, the tramway company, perhaps surprisingly, being one of them. Shrewd observers may well have realised then that the writing was on the wall for the Sheerness trams, but perhaps the British Electric Traction Company recognised that it couldn't afford to be left behind in the race to establish omnibus routes.

During July there were reports of overcrowding on the 'buses, charges of reckless driving and speeding which, in one instance, caused serious injury to a workman. Such unregulated chaos may well have worsened had it not been for the interruption caused by the war which somewhat curtailed the excesses of this infant enterprise, at least for the time being.

It would appear that not everyone was so convinced that there would be a war with Germany, for ambitious schemes were still coming forward. In June the 'Minster-on-Sea Hotel Company' was launched, inviting speculators to buy shares in this promising new venture which anticipated greater glories for this spot in Sheppey. Any advancement of the share issue, let alone the works were soon pre-empted, however, by the declaration of war on 4th August. There followed the usual patriotic nonsense in the press as well as the shameful harassment of innocent individuals. Mr Losel, a respected Sheerness photographer and resident there for over forty years, was seized while in the town with his camera by a zealous constable. The unfortunate man was eventually forced to leave the country.

The effect upon the railways of Sheppey was gradual. In November the press announced that the 'Mile Town' [Sheerness-on-Sea] station would be closed other than for goods traffic, whereas the light railway would assume greater importance with the aviation facilities at Eastchurch. The SE & CR promised to keep as many trains running as possible, but the public were given a stern warning: 'Owing to the military requirements the Company may find it necessary to cancel any train at short notice'. In spite of the confident predictions as to the outcome of this 'war to end all wars', shadows of doubt were cast in most people's mind. How long would the conflict really last? Could Sheerness and Eastchurch be bombed by the Zeppelins? How many Sheppeyites might die in the fields of France and Belgium and would life ever be quite the same again in the 'Unknown Paradise'?

'At the end of the street stand the men, who always do stand to look at flowing water.' — Arthur Lewis. The lazy waters of the Medway lap the shoreline at Queenborough where craft are dotted about in this view towards the pier. *Author's collection*

A closer view of Queenborough pier, taken on the same day, where the funnels of a cross-channel steamer peep above the buildings of the ex-LC & DR station which once rivalled the SER's Port Victoria. *Author's collection*

CHAPTER FIVE

THE UNKNOWN PARADISE

Edwardian Queenborough, where the High Street led on to the shoreline, and the River Medway which beckoned idle passers-by to simply stand and stare. *Author's collection*

FOR those who'd travelled by train to this Kentish isle, a journey through the 'Unknown Paradise' would commence at Queenborough station. Here, large nameboards upon both platforms proclaimed: 'Queenborough – Change for Sheppey Light Railway'.

The station buildings, even in Edwardian days, were certainly striking and even somewhat awesome. Their appearance was vaguely reminiscent of the ecclesiastical, the roofs having extremely high and exaggerated pitches. The windows had rounded-tops rather than the more pleasing pointed arches of the gothic revival which the LC & DR marvellously adopted to such striking effect. However, since the station at Queenborough was, of course, built by the S & SR Co, this explains the uniqueness of the railway buildings on the island. I do not know whether devotees of Victorian architecture would praise or dismiss these peculiar buildings, but I think John Minnis, in his enjoyable book on SE & CR country stations, rather succinctly hit the nail on the head: 'The proportions of the building were, on the whole, nightmarish, giving the gimcrack look of a tin tabernacle'.

To obtain a glimpse of Queenborough itself, during the heyday of the Sheppey Light Railway, is a little difficult since most contemporary guide books dismiss the place in a few sentences. Comments are invariably restricted to its numerous industries and associations with cross-channel trade. Thankfully, Arthur Lewis, writing in his book *The Kent Coast*, published in 1911 is more forthcoming:

> 'Its main street is rather quaint – large signs sway before numerous inns – the rich red brick houses, of a colour that modern bricks cannot achieve, and others of wood, are of various heights'.

Glancing at Edwardian views of Queenborough the scenes he fondly describes are indeed easily found, where rows of pleasing solid-looking terraced houses, built of local clay and as yet mercifully unblemished by today's 'improvements', bring simple pleasure to the eye. Here is an example of the quintessential English working town – a random but harmonious medley of brick and clapboard, which has naturally evolved over many years. Side by side stand the humble and the rather grand in a fashion that is nowadays impossible to recreate. Smart iron railings, elegant streetlamps and well-tended gardens border authentically developed roads which lead past a rich variety of little shops and houses. Some of these roads lead directly to the waterfront, the scene quite sensitively described by Arthur Lewis:

> 'At the end of the street stand the men, who always do stand to look at flowing water. The water is quite like the sea and every kind of craft may be seen rising and falling on the waves. To the right (eastwards) a gay little flower-garden borders the water, and beside this there begins the long sea-wall, which proceeds past marshy fields and Queenborough Railway Pier (where the Flushing boats start) to the Admiralty Pier at Sheerness. One or two factories are seen inland

The striking buildings erected at Queenborough at the opening of the first railway on the island. In the bay is one of the 3rd class vestibuled carriages used on the Sheppey Light Railway.
Collection Martin Hawkins

Railmotor No. 1 caught in the late afternoon rays of sunshine while the staff at Queenborough load up with luggage. Someone was evidently planning a break on the sandy shoreline at Leysdown judging by the canvas deckchair packed along with suitcases.
The Railway Magazine

The view towards Sittingbourne, shortly before the addition of the iron footbridge which was not just a welcome convenience, but a useful asset for all the little boys who liked to watch the trains go by!
Collection Reg Randell

A rooftop panorama across industrious Queenborough where the smoke from numerous chimneys was a landmark for many miles across the flat marshes of the island.
Collection Martin Hawkins

on the way – how strange the white smoke out of their chimneys looks against a dark grey sky.'

Returning to the station, those who had alighted from the Sheerness train made their way along the platform to cross the railway to reach the bay where the Leysdown train awaited them. Initially, passengers had to traverse the main line by way of a foot crossing at the northern end of the platforms, but it wasn't too long before safety requirements encouraged the SE & CR to erect an iron footbridge at the southern end. This bridge provided the perfect vantage point for dawdling children to linger so they might watch the departure of the southbound trains before skipping down the stairs to join the rest of the family. Whether it was an ancient LC & DR tank, the railmotor's diminutive engine, or the familiar friend *Little Tich*, they all provided a moment of cautious wonderment for countless young lads who customarily wandered up to peer into the cab. Braving the daunting aspect, wary youngsters gradually edged nearer to these seemingly living machines which sweated hot oil, while the heat from the boiler and firebox radiated around. Scalding droplets of water fizzled and spluttered out from crevices around the motion, trailing steam as they disappeared onto the greasy, cinder-strewn track below. The noise of the blower and more so the sudden deafening roar as safety valves lifted, gave an all too vivid indication of the terrifying pent-up power of these harnessed mechanical beasts, which seemed so impatient to be let loose.

Safe within the comfort and security of the somewhat grimy and malodorous rake of stock dating from 1887, the guard's 'right-away' whistle would usually be echoed by an acknowledgement from the engine up ahead which coaxed the line of elderly carriages into motion. Ever so slowly, with couplings creaking, the train would be gently eased out of the bay and over the points which guided the train eastwards and onto the single line.

On almost level land, the curving track led the train along a shallow embankment where points at either end of a short loop caused each set of wheels to clatter. The trailing smoke from factory chimneys and the pots on terraces of houses gradually receded, whilst Sheerness bordered the horizon from the left-hand compartment window. Along the immediate vicinity of the line, in the rich green fields on either side, sheep continued their tedious grazing, unperturbed by the regular beat and resounding wheels of the passing train. Lonely farmsteads and isolated cottages would pass by as the train began to pick up a little more speed. However, no sooner had the journey begun then it was time to stop as steam was shut off and the brakes applied. Up ahead, the gates across the Halfway House Road would be closed against the road, whilst in the days before the Great War there was often a tram to be seen swaying along the open road from Sheerness. Once over the crossing, the train entered the single platform of Sheerness East station which was built on the northern side of the railway.

Sheerness East station was the nearest the Sheppey Light Railway ever ventured to what might be termed the 'capital' of the island. In many respects it was something of a misnomer since the town was a good mile away, but that kind of drawback never did seem to bother builders of light railways. In spite of this, the station was undoubtedly one of the busiest and most prosperous on the line, thanks to the tramway which was greeted with such hostility by the railway. Indeed, the Sheppey Light owed a great debt to the trams which brought it load upon load of noisy daytrippers, excited holidaymakers, ambitious prospectors and grateful locals.

From its humble origin as 'a mere swamp', Sheerness gradually evolved into one of the most interesting places in Kent and it was certainly an enthralling district to visit around the turn of the century. Like neighbouring Queenborough, its streets were bordered with a fascinating mixture of buildings, if anything even more distinctive and varied than seems possible. Along its busy thoroughfares children of all ages played together, sat upon the kerbstones or in the middle of the road until a tram came rumbling and hissing along to send then scattering. Once again, however, it should be left to Arthur Lewis to best describe the scene which greeted the Edwardian explorers:

> 'Sheerness straggles along the water-side for some distance, the dockyard occupying the shore for some time after the pier is passed. The long street which succeeds is the main street of what is known as Blue Town – it is well-furnished with lodging houses intended for "sailor's homes", though most announce that they are open to the public except on Sundays, and it contains many timber houses, which resemble many to be found in the sailors' quarters of Whitstable and Folkestone. The long sea-wall of Sheerness-on-Sea now begins, and for the first time the coast faces the open sea, with no hint of an opposite shore. If the weather is rough, the waves wash over the wall, and this is perhaps why so many of the houses are placed with their backs to the sea. On a windy day, for anyone who likes to see a rough sea and to enjoy a blow, the wall offers attractions – the convulsive swells of the waves, fathomless, incalculable, the occasional lines of curling foam reflected in the indescribable dark green of the waters, the veins of light on the waters below cracks in the clouds, are before you.'

After a speedy ride by electric tram from the Coronation clock tower and along the Halfway House Road, locals and those who had come from further afield via the Port Victoria – Sheerness route were deposited at Sheerness East. Along the way the Sheppey Race Course was passed, which could be easily reached by either train or tram. Eastbound visitors alighting from the trams had but a few steps to take before purchasing tickets for Minster, Eastchurch or Leysdown. The station building and indeed the entire facilities, might be accurately described as 'pure Stephens', for from the outset they bore all the hallmarks of the remarkable man's achievements. Railway engineering on a shoe-string budget was an art which, it is acknowledged, he singularly perfected where no expenditure other than the bare minimum was made. The platform facing at Sheerness East, in common with others on the line, consisted of redundant sleepers positioned vertically, with horizontal members bolted along the

A precious glimpse of Sheerness, full of atmosphere. The street was a playground and the kerbs and lamp posts formed part of the games children played. Even the trams were fun and many a wayward lad was ticked-off for sitting astride a bicycle while hanging on to the swaying cars. Collection R. Cullen

top edge. A wooden coping was added to border the clinker and gravel platform surfacing. At the rear, a wooden trellis fencing sufficed, whilst two or three oil lamps were fixed upon wooden posts for illumination at dusk. A solitary wooden nameboard and a simple flat bench or two completed the sparse furbishments. The station building followed a style adopted by Stephens from the SER who made such savings whenever necessary. Basically, the structure comprised a timber framing, with a wooden panelled interior and corrugated iron sheeting affixed to the exterior walls and roof. However, the SER stations built in this manner, on the Hawkhurst branch and the Canterbury extension of the Elham Valley Line, were much larger affairs, with the roofs extended to form platform canopies. The derivation of the style applied by Stephens on the Sheppey Light saw the creation of a much smaller and slightly cruder building. Here, a traditional roof was constructed, with a separate platform canopy supported by wooden pillars. It has to be said, however, that they were probably quite adequate for the purpose, apart from the lack of proper public conveniences. At the eastern end of Sheerness East station there was a gents' urinal, but curiously there was no 'Ladies Room'. Inside the building there was a ticket office, a waiting room and a roader office where goods consignments were sorted. Across the railway a modest goods yard with cattle pens was provided to deal with the local agricultural traffic. In the very early days a set of points existed at the eastern end of the siding, thus creating a loop, but the SE & CR removed this at some stage.

For those with an interest in all the innovative developments in transport, a glance over the platform fence brought a view of

A summer's view to distant Sheerness from daisy-strewn Furze Hill. The hamlet of Halfway is in the foreground, whilst the course of the Sheppey Light Railway may be detected by the line of telegraph poles running across the centre of the picture.
Collection Martin Hawkins

the Sheerness Tramway Company's cars weaving their way along the road behind the station to and from their depot. Indeed, much interest was shown in April 1903 when a conducted tour was given to show off the new electrical power generating apparatus.

Starting away from the station on a rising gradient of 1 in 89, the trains soon reached level ground before a short fall and then a climb of 1 in 75 as the line followed the undulating green pastures of the rural district. The railway continued along a shallow embankment and in an almost straight line before running over Scraps Gate level crossing. A few hundred yards further a brief stop was made at East Minster-on-Sea.

Whereas Sheerness East might be considered a misnomer, East Minster-on-Sea was distinctly misleading since it was actually *west* of Minster. It can only be surmised that the company didn't want to cause confusion with West Minster which lies between

A train for Queenborough, comprising the vestibuled set, waiting at Sheerness East in the days before the line was amalgamated into the SE & CR.
Collection Reg Randell

This charming Edwardian card of East Minster illustrates the original narrow level crossing. The halt and crossing keeper's hut can be seen behind the paling fence.
Collection Martin Hawkins

Queenborough and Sheerness. Evenso, it must surely have caused some consternation throughout the life of the railway for those who remained on board at Minster-on-Sea and then found themselves at Brambledown or Eastchurch. The logic is reminiscent of 'Oh! Mr Porter' and it is not difficult to imagine a character in the likeness of Will Hay confusingly explaining the company's reasoning to bewildered and irate passengers.

For the first few years the trains didn't bother to call here except when a special occasion, such as a land sale, made it more convenient. Matters improved slightly following the introduction of the steam railcars, but even then passengers were required to ask the guard to set them down, or signal to the driver of an approaching train. Thus, the facilities offered here were every bit as meagre as might well be expected. A very short platform (later extended by the SE & CR) bordered the track on the southern side, upon which stood a small shelter containing a wooden bench around the three walls. East Minster-on-Sea perhaps epitomised what might be described as the rustic charm of the long-lost light railways. It was nothing more than a roadside halt at a remote level crossing, provided to serve the scattered community and probably patronised by less than half a dozen passengers a day, or maybe even a week. Here it stood, isolated and desolate, with the railway winding away into the distance. Invariably, there was a long wait for the next train. Happily, though, the stranded wayfarer with an hour or two to kill was not left to kick his heels at East Minster, listening only to the cries of marsh birds or for the hopeful tell-tale signs of an approaching train. Just across the line was a wonderful oasis in the form of a general store which served teas, much to the probable delight of those who craved the satisfaction of 'the cup that cheers'.

East Minster-on-Sea station in the mid-1930s, showing how the platform was extended and improved by the SE & CR. This view, which is towards the Leysdown direction, also depicts new and much wider level crossing gates.
H. A. Vallance

The village of Minster, upon its hilltop setting, and spreading out across the once empty fields and meadows.
Author's collection

For half a mile beyond East Minster, the railway rose on a steady gradient of 1 in 77 until Minster-on-Sea station was reached. It was such a short distance that trains in the opposite direction must have almost rolled the few hundred yards between stops with the regulator barely open.

The station stood on the northern side of the line, facing a small yard with a siding and cattle pens. Facilities inside the station were similar to Sheerness East. Half a mile away stands Minster, upon a hilltop setting, the highest in the island, which Arthur Mee once described as 'The Marvel of Sheppey'. In his series of books *The King's England*, published in the 1930s, he is quite scathing about twentieth century development at Minster:

'MINSTER-IN-SHEPPEY: The marvel of the Isle of Sheppey, it is one of the marvels of all England, too. A tasteless world has grown up around it, and we may be thankful for imagination as we walk about here. This place grew out of a green hill. This gem was once set in a silver sea; now they have surrounded it with ugliness, have piled up higgledy-piggledy bricks, have covered the earth with

A quiet corner of Minster when the private motor car had yet to make its presence known.
Author's collection

bungalows and petty things, and left the wonder of Sheppey alone with its past.'

The 'on-Sea' part of the station name was, as might be expected, something of an exaggeration for the perplexed traveller, desirous of wetting the toes, faced a wearying tramp of almost two miles before the water's edge was reached. Along the winding lanes and on to the delightfully-named Pigtail Corner, Edwardian visitors wandered unless they were able to afford to hire a 'fly' or motor car. Down winding East End Lane, past the neatly-tended gardens of homesteads and bungalows dotted between the wayside hedgerows, till, at last, a parting in the bushes rewarded them with their first glimpse of the sea. Rural, unspoilt and natural, might best describe the hidden stretch of Kentish coastline greeting expectant day trippers, but where was Mr Ramuz's fine hotel? Where were the elegant villas to accompany this latest enterprise and what had happened to the plans to build the world's longest pier which was to rival brash and boastful Southend? Perhaps those who squatted upon the shore with bored and restless children may have wondered likewise, or maybe day-dreamers upon the cliffs were thankful for its rustic quietude.

It was probably just as well that on the way home the final trek to the station was downhill. Station Road led past newly-erected bungalows, some of weatherboard, others built in brick, whilst pebbledash appeared the vogue. In spite of the unrelenting march of these rural retreats, Minster-on-Sea station remained in isolation, facing out across the broad sweep of cornfields and meadows towards the distant glinting Swale. On a drowsy summer's afternoon it would not have been uncommon for the intending traveller to wonder if there was anyone at the station. Momentarily, a welcome cooling breeze might stir and rustle the leaves on the wayside elms, bringing the distant sounds of bleating sheep from an indiscernible spot somewhere in the shimmering haze beyond. Apart from the chorus of unseen grasshoppers along the dry, dusty roadside verges where nasty-looking flying insects busied themselves upon the common blossoms, little else was heard. At the station, all was silent save, perhaps, for a cage left under the welcome shade of the canopy where restless chickens occasionally stirred. In the hot sunshine the rails would periodically creak, while the heat radiated back from the platform and the dull, flat paint peeling on the corrugated iron building. This deserted scene was commonplace on all the light railways, but as the time approached for the train's arrival stirrings inside would prompt an enquiry for a ticket or a connection at Queenborough. No doubt laying aside the folded newspaper that had shielded eyes for forty winks, the porter might well stretch and scratch his head before checking the clock upon the wall. For a brief period the tiny station would

Here they came at weekends, down winding East End Lane, to reach the north coast of the island and with little to do but sit upon the lonely beach and gaze across the Thames Estuary.
Author's collection

In typical isolation, the light railway station at Minster-on-Sea is seen at the end of this lane and leading past these newly erected bungalows which were quite the vogue. *Author's collection*

A momentary pause for the camera by the porter and young lad with his horse at Minster-on-Sea in this rare early Edwardian postcard of the station and yard. *Collection Martin Hawkins*

The beauty of Sheppey was greatly enhanced by hundreds of lovely elms which once graced the byways throughout the island. Nowadays, almost all have fallen victim to disease and are no more. Here, we may only ponder how wonderful it once looked in this exquisite scene showing the road from Eastchurch to Queenborough, with Brambledown Halt glimpsed on the right.

Collection Martin Hawkins

This enchanting aspect of rural Brambledown Halt, looking towards Leysdown in the 1930s, truly captures the atmosphere of the Sheppey Light.
H. A. Vallance

echo with the sound of hollow footsteps upon the bare wooden floorboards as other people began to arrive. Once the train and its passengers had departed, Minster-on-Sea would be left undisturbed once again to enjoy its summertime slumbers.

Pulling away from Minster, the railway resumed climbing at 1 in 70 towards Stickfast Lane crossing where, for a short distance, the line levelled out. Here the track began to swing southwards, descending at 1 in 74 within a shallow cutting. A few yards further the platform at Brambledown Halt came into view from the left-hand carriage window. Standing on the northern side of the line, the wayside wooden halt was entirely of SE & CR origin. A traditional waiting shed stood upon the platform to give refuge to those who had braved the sudden squall of spring or autumn, or the constant drizzle of a November day, as they walked along the unsheltered lanes. There was little else except for a nameboard, a row of fire buckets and two oil lamps, although how often the platform was regularly illuminated is a mystery.

Once across the 'B' road which ran between Minster and Eastchurch, the railway started curving eastwards as it headed directly for Leysdown. After Newhook Farm crossing, the line then began to run through some of the most picturesque countryside which the island had to offer, most noticeably in springtime when frail pink orchard blossom dusted the gentle landscape which spread out both sides. Here, the locomotive's steady beat would become more discernible as the railway climbed to reach the summit of the whole line. Having passed

The railway near Newhook Farm, seen sweeping across the fertile fields to Eastchurch, whilst the hangars belonging to the aerodrome are perched on the hilltop horizon.
Denis Cullum

Grove Siding. Taken from the 25-inch Ordnance Survey of 1907. Crown Copyright reserved.

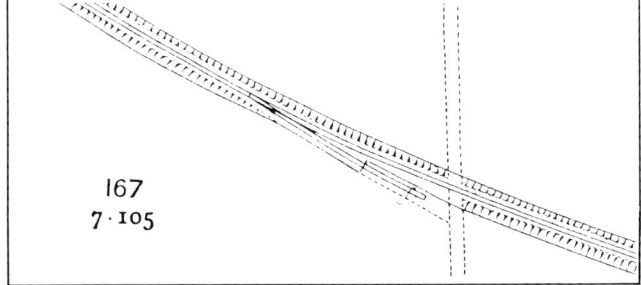

by a small siding at Grove Farm on the south side, it was only half a mile before Eastchurch station was reached.

Eastchurch was the most important stopping place on the route between Queenborough and Leysdown. It was also the wintertime terminus for passenger trains during the early years of the Sheppey Light Railway. The station possessed a fully-signalled loop and would have been capable of taking a second platform similar, for example, to that provided at Biddenden on the Kent & East Sussex Railway. It would appear that Colonel Pringle, who inspected the line in 1901, was under the impression that Eastchurch was to have been used as a passing place, for passenger trains. At a later inspection, in 1917, he was rather critical over the lack of catch points being otherwise provided.

Apart from a rather expansive goods yard in front of the station, there was also a large area to the rear which was used to auction livestock. Upon the platform a traditional 'Sheppey Light' building rested, whilst the station benefited from the later improvements and additions provided by the SE & CR.

The village of Eastchurch stands a little over a half a mile away to the north and those prepared to walk up Pump Hill were rewarded with a glimpse of simple, honest English village life. In summer the pleasant, quiet and sun-parched dusty streets led past the one-time familiar huddle of shops where essentials were purchased, while pleasantries and the odd item of gossip were freely exchanged. Large blinds shaded most shop windows from the fierce midday sun, while a faded canvas curtain often gently swayed in the soft breeze, stretched across the beckoning doorway of the local teashop, keeping the interior cool and welcoming. From within came the distinctive rattle of teacups and cutlery, whilst the smell of freshly-baked scones, cakes and bread proved irresistible to most passers-by. Inside, Sheppey excursionists enjoyed simple, honest fare, poached eggs perhaps, or boiled ham with plain buttered bread or Kentish huffkins. Home-made scones and jam, with strong, hot tea in china cups would then come through from the back kitchens. The cool gloom of these often low-ceilinged, unpretentious tea parlours were welcome retreats for the wearied who'd walked further than they'd intended. In a corner stood a rack or bentwood stand for walking canes, straw boaters and fancy hats bedecked with feathers, flowers or imitation fruit, while upon a yellowed wall the clock slowly ticked away the passing hours. Often beyond the kitchen door, in the brilliant, sun-drenched back

Top: An early view of Eastchurch, taken about 1905, looking towards Queenborough and showing the original signal used to control the running road and loop siding. *Above:* The construction of the Sheppey Light Railway encouraged further development nearer the line. Here, smart terraced houses line the road leading to the station. *The Railway Magazine and Collection Martin Hawkins*

Drowsy Eastchurch on a sunny summer's afternoon. This 1920s view wonderfully captures the quiet scene which greeted the wanderer of wayside villages and hamlets.

Author's collection

The breezy heights at Eastchurch cliffs where came Londoners in search of weekend breaks and a respite from the heat and dust of the city. Others came to settle here permanently and, in doing so, created a ramshackle hamlet of bungalows and shacks upon the once-lonely downland. *Author's collection*

Eastchurch during the 1930s, showing the goods yard and loop siding and the ever-present elms which graced the landscape and distant horizons towards Leysdown.
H. A. Vallance

yard, the shop's cat periodically yawned and stretched, before settling down again beneath a shady spot to continue her slumbers and dreams.

Apart from these wonderfully ordinary teashops, there were generally ample establishments for those desirous of something stronger. In Eastchurch for example a rasping thirst might equally be quenched either at the 'Castle Inn' or the delightfully-named 'Crooked Billet' which advertised 'Kent's Best'. The dull murmur of conversation, interspersed by the sounds of chinking glasses and money changing hands, was all that disturbed the peace when such a state was once so valued and respected.

Those who were more adventuresome were free to explore the highways and byways of this district, perhaps wandering as far as the lonely cliffs, a mile or so beyond. Here, came city-dwellers seeking the precious quietude, arriving in their shiny motor cars which bounced and swayed protestingly over the uneven tracks and grassy hillocks before pulling-up outside the hired weekend chalet. Who knows what sometimes went on behind the little lace-curtained windows of these conveniently secret hideaways?

Returning to Eastchurch station, there was often time for a quick 'cuppa' at the house by the crossing which thoughtfully provided teas. Gazing eastwards from the platform, the gradient of 1 in 73 towards Leysdown was most noticeable as the railway cut a gentle swathe through the soft fold of rising ground to the east. Fortunately, the steep grades along the Sheppey Light were never long enough to tax the limited power of the railmotors which, on a busy day with the trailer car attached, must have struggled to haul the load, especially when there was no opportunity to obtain a run at the bank.

At the top of the incline leading away from Eastchurch, the summit of the whole line was reached. From here it was mostly a gradual descent towards Leysdown. Holford Siding passed by on the south side of the railway, just before the train swept over the occupation crossing at Old Rides. Shutting off steam, the train crew prepared to stop at Harty Road Halt which stood in splendid isolation amidst the wide and open wind-beaten fields. A

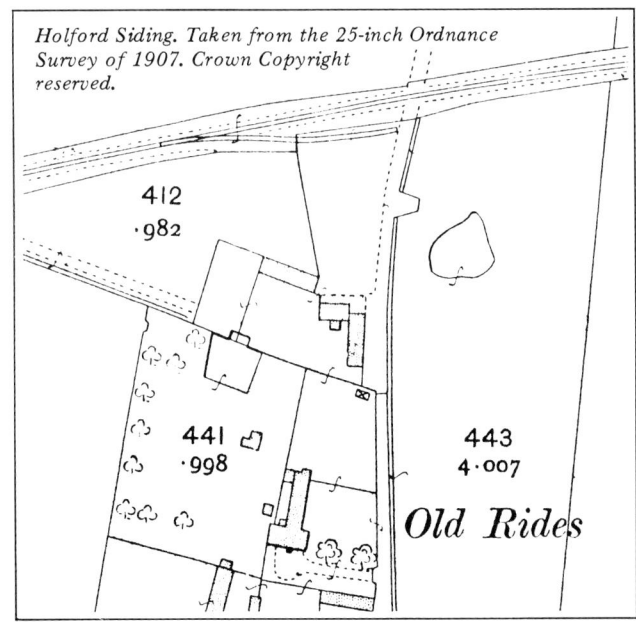

Holford Siding. Taken from the 25-inch Ordnance Survey of 1907. Crown Copyright reserved.

Along the winding road that led to Leysdown, rows of elms bordered the fields and in high summer shaded the cyclist or pedestrian from the sun. It was a long trek to Harty Road Halt which stood at the end of this beckoning lane.
Collection Martin Hawkins

How many people regularly used Harty Road Halt is a mystery, for here it stood by the trackside in total isolation amidst the open fields. This 1930s view, looking in the direction of Leysdown, depicts the humble wooden platform and small shelter. *H. A. Vallance*

squat wooden platform and hut, similar to that at Brambledown, bordered the line on the south. However, it was probably more than adequate for the few souls who used it, the farmers' wives on market days and, in the '20s and '30s, the ramblers who took up the current rage and eagerly ventured forth either from smoke-bound cities or leafier suburbia. Arthur Mee noted:

> 'HARTY: It is a place of solitude. The bus calls once a week; the school has sixteen children; the lanes are so quiet that fifty sparrows will fly up from the road in front of a car.'

At Harty Road the guard would clamber down, as was his duty elsewhere, to open the wooden gates which barred the way. Having pulled slowly forward, the train drifted along at walking pace until, with gates closed once more behind, the guard hurried along to climb aboard. The siding at Harty Road was also on the south side, on the Leysdown side of the crossing, where the pick-up goods disturbed the silence for a short time on odd days throughout the week.

Picking up a gentle, rocking motion once more, the locomotive's whistle was given the obligatory blast on the approach to Mustards Road level crossing, then again, just half a mile further, when nearing Frog's Island crossing. At this point the regulator was eased off in preparation for journey's end as Leysdown station swung into view up ahead. Passing the protecting home signal, the train would clatter over the points leading into the goods yard and loop siding before entering the platform which ran along the northern side of the line.

Leysdown station was the largest on the line and the building, although of similar pattern, likewise differed in size. At the western end, forming a lean-to, was a covered gents' lavatory, but, here again, the need for a 'ladies' convenience surprisingly

The guard of a Leysdown train closing the gates across the railway once more while the train waits for him to clamber aboard.
Pamlin Prints

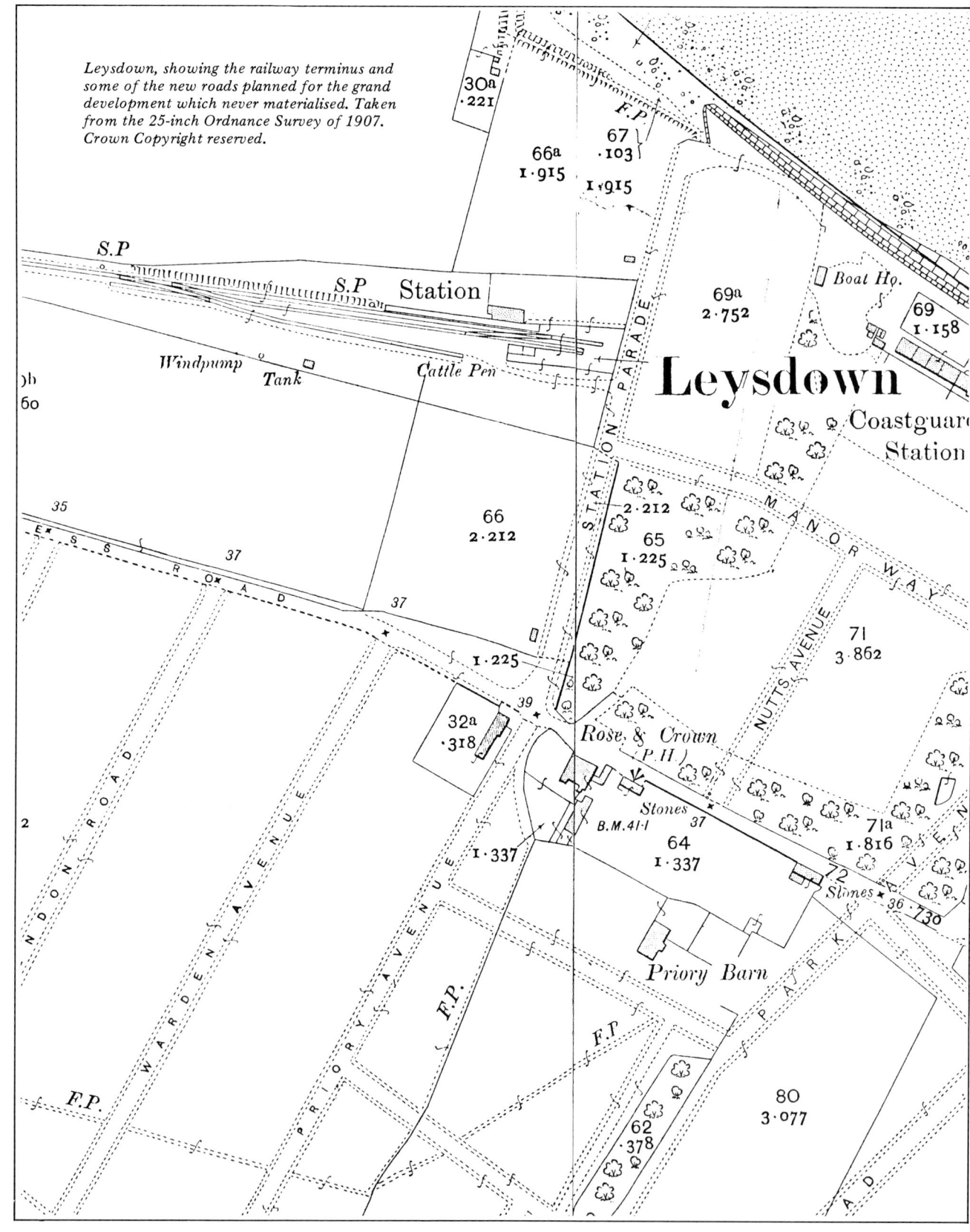

Leysdown, showing the railway terminus and some of the new roads planned for the grand development which never materialised. Taken from the 25-inch Ordnance Survey of 1907. Crown Copyright reserved.

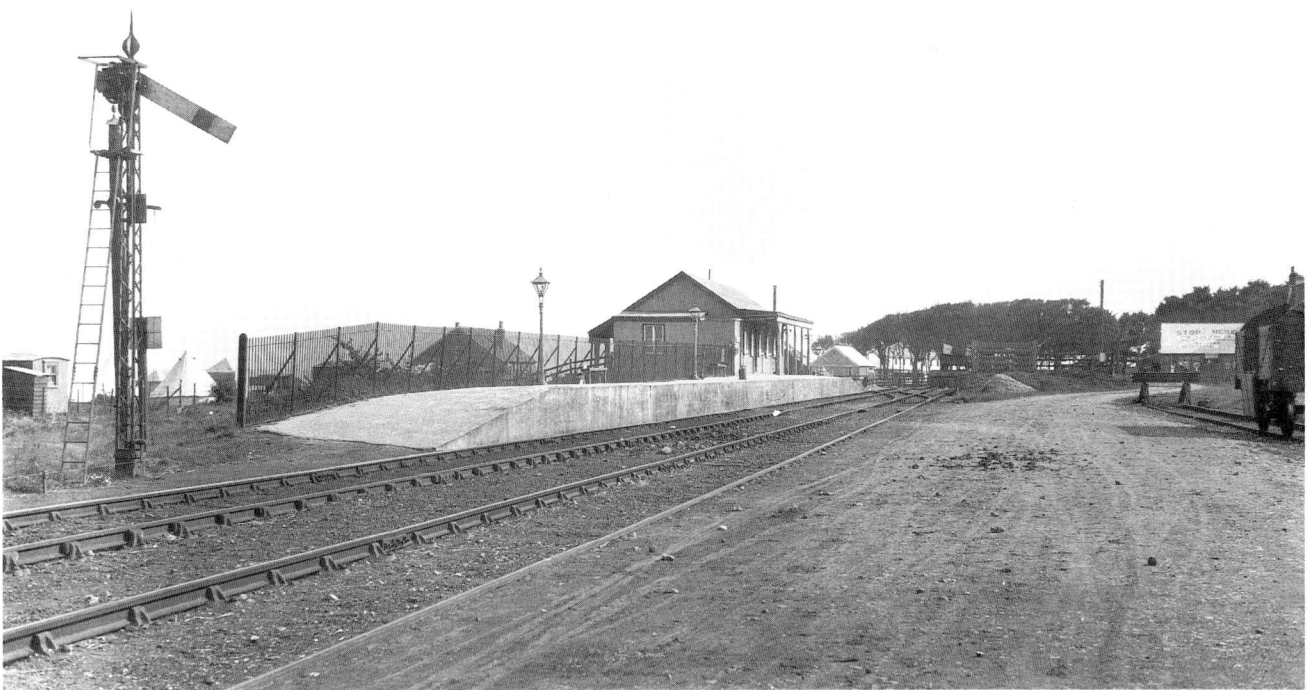

This 1930s photograph of Leysdown station illustrates the improvements which were effected by the SE & CR, namely the concrete-faced platforms, LC & DR pattern signals, iron fencing and lamp posts.   *H. A. Vallance*

never entered the heads of the light railway builders. Inside the main building were the stores, waiting room and booking office, whilst across the line a spacious horse and carriage dock, together with cattle pens stood at the entrance to the goods yard. Towards the western end of the yard, set back from the sidings and on the perimeter of railway land, rose the water tank which the SE & CR erected upon a stout brick housing. The water stand for filling locomotive tanks stood adjacent to the loop line where, nearby, an engine pit was sunk.

Not unexpectedly, the SE & CR carried out similar improvements here throughout the early years of its administration. The wooden latticed fencing and lamp posts soon gave way to sturdier iron replacements, whereas the original wooden-posted signals made way for ex-LC & DR examples. Whilst these improvements were welcome and necessary, they did, however, dispel the air of individuality which specialised the character of the Sheppey Light Railway.

Leaving the station, either by the ramp or the twin flights of steps into the approach road, it was only a few yards to walk to reach the grandly-named 'Station Parade' to find what Leysdown-on-Sea might have to offer. In the days before the Great War the place was certainly quiet and rural, still awaiting the promised development. Indeed, there was disappointment for those who expected another Southend. Arthur Lewis, who came here in Edwardian times, wrote:

> 'The terminus of the light railway from Queenborough is between Warden Point and Shellness Point at Leysdown. Here I would advise pedestrians to turn a few steps inland and refresh themselves at the "Rose and Crown". For the coast of Sheppey is not over-supplied with places of refreshment.'

In the field behind Leysdown station 'fully furnished' bell tents were hired out to weekenders and holidaymakers during the season.   *Collection Martin Hawkins*

He continues with his experiences there:

> 'Leysdown consists of an abandoned boarding house, "Sea View", which still asks on a notice-board for lodgers, though it is locked up, unfurnished, and deserted, a railway station, the inn, and about three coast-guard houses near the sea, so you will not expect the inn to provide French cooking. Still its charges are proportionately low, so that I ate a meat tea, supper, and breakfast, and went to bed there for 3s 2d.'

The sea and gritty sandy shore are but a short walk from the station and the excited children of generations past would, no doubt, have been quite content with building sandcastles, paddling in the murky, speckled water and exploring the jetsam tossed up along the water's edge. For the more determined and purposeful, a walk through the 'Unknown Paradise' to Warden Point was certainly rewarding once the steep climb up the craggy and crumbling, ruddy-brown cliffs to the summit had been achieved. Here, on a clear and beautiful day, a perfect view could be obtained of forgotten Leysdown way below, with the trains coming and going upon the light railway. A breathtaking vista across the mouth of the lazy Swale, led on to the rolling hills of mainland Kent and industrious Whitstable, just across the water. Perhaps, though, the final word should be left to Arthur Lewis who best described the scene at that time:

> 'Warden Point is a fine headland – I saw it recently as a faded green headland with rust-red edges presented to a pearly sea-woods of a heavier green curled over its summit – the sky above held a dark cloud with a silver base. The cliffs diminish on the farther side, and the sea is bordered by a beach of shells and an embankment on the other side of which is a swamp of richly coloured dull-green grasses between which are pools reflecting the grass stalks and the grey sky. The beach of shells continues to Shellness Point. When the sea goes out it leaves a wide stretch of shallow water on the sands, and a bright busy sky is reflected cheerfully into the shallows below.'

This pleasant tree-lined avenue was also known by the rather grand title of Station Parade, where nearby shops maintained well-stocked shelves piled high with all the necessary items for an enjoyable day at the seaside. The entrance to Leysdown station is opposite the parked vehicle.
Author's collection

Sadly, all the trees in this view have long since disappeared due to disease. In happier and more verdant times the Rose & Crown nestled among these leafy boughs and tempted Arthur Lewis to stay here in 1911.
Collection Martin Hawkins

Whilst many came by train, others motored down in the 1920s in cars which bounced and whined across the uneven ground and tussocks which bordered the lonely shoreline at Shellness.
Author's collection

The simple pleasures of a day at the seaside in the 1920s may well be imagined in this evocative view towards Warden Bay of the seashore at Leysdown.
Author's collection

This marvellous panorama taken from the crumbling cliffs at Warden Bay shows the tiny seaside resort of Leysdown slumbering in the warmth of the midsummer sunshine. On the horizon is the mainland of Kent, just across the Swale, whereas the station, water tower and wagons in the sidings may all be seen across the centre of the picture. *Author's collection*

Looking down Station Parade on a bright summer's morning, with day trippers arriving by train.

Collection Martin Hawkins

Whatever the weather, here they came in their hundreds to sit and play on the sands or splash around in the sea.

Collection Martin Hawkins

The busy docks at Sheerness were always an interesting place to visit. Here, a twin-funnelled paddle steamer nudges the quayside in this view taken around the turn of the century.
Author's collection

The bystanders on the sea wall at Sheerness seem to be more interested in the cameraman than tramcar No. 7 which is rumbling along Marine Parade. The unusual method of current collection through the sprung bow is clearly shown.
Collection Richard Cullen

CHAPTER SIX

LIVE AT LEYSDOWN!

THE Great War occasioned a watershed in the history of the Sheppey Light Railway, as well as marking a sea-change in British history, customs and social affairs. Up until the last summer of peace in 1914 the little railway, which meandered across the gently undulating countryside of this Kentish isle to the tiny seaside resort of Leysdown, enjoyed a modicum of security and prosperity. These years, between the coronation of George V and the outbreak of war, were to mark the twilight of the great railway age. This era, which lasted for almost a whole century, brought with it undreamt of advancements in travelling, commerce, industrial development and social freedoms. The arrival of the tramways and, soon after, the light railways, brought to ordinary folk an affordable means of moving around, whilst to local traders, farmers and businessmen they were a boon. Throughout their heyday these iron roads seemed untouchable, as permanent as the districts, communities and landscapes through which they passed. Indeed, everyone thought of them as immutable, a part of the very fabric of life. Yet, as we know dearly to our cost, the light railways, tramways and even irreplaceable sections of the great national railway system, were subjected to destructive and thoughtless policies of successive postwar generations. However, the demise of the Sheppey Light Railway, along with many other similar lines, began as long ago as the dark days between 1914–18.

At the commencement of the war there was much coming and going around Sheerness. The everyday bustle of human activity in the High Street was enlivened and heightened by the nervous talk of war, whilst everyone felt the need to vent an opinion. The clattering of iron-rimmed cartwheels and horses' hooves upon the cobbled thoroughfares added to this sense of urgency. In the dockyards the scene was one of almost constant activity as supplies, guns and munitions were unloaded from countless railway trucks. These goods soon disappeared once more into the darkness of the ships' holds as the combined efforts of machinery and muscle toiled hour after hour. Huge, coarse hemp ropes, steel cords and massive chains were fastened to the stout and stumpy iron capstans where constant use had burnished them to a glinting patina. These lines restrained ships which seemed impatient to be freed from their shackles as they rose and fell on the swell, nudging the virisdescent, slime-draped baulks of the quaysides. Great, grey and towering four-funnelled warships, terrifying in their aspect, could be seen plying to and fro, far out in the Thames Reach, with huge black clouds sometimes belching and trailing from their smokestacks as they swung full ahead and steamed out into the German Ocean. Elsewhere, small steam tugs and other craft criss-crossed each other at the mouth of the Medway which bore the dauntingly grim, warring leviathans to and from His Majesty's dockyards.

Sheerness was designated a restricted area, as were other towns and localities in Kent with strategic or military associations. The public bars must have buzzed with one topic only as voices were periodically raised above the din. Across smoke-filled rooms it is likely that some heads shook in silent and fearful foreboding, whilst others who were anxious to 'have a go' found the numbing alcohol all too easily loosening their tongues and their bravado.

In many ways it appears to have been a rather peculiar time, for no one knew quite what to expect. The initial fears of massive aerial bombardment with the aid of the Zeppelins proved unfounded. One contemporary postcard 'commemorated' a raid, tracing the course of the enemy aircraft upon a map of Sheppey and boasting only one casualty – an unfortunate blackbird. In spite of such fervent attempts to boost morale, there was not much comfort for those whose loved ones were dying in their thousands in the hell-holes of the Somme.

While such carnage was allowed to rage unchecked across the English Channel, in sharpest contrast rural Sheppey retained its timeless peace and beauty. At the end of yet another hot, drowsy day in late summer, it was possible to sit upon a quiet hillside in evening's afterglow and reflect upon those sad times. Gazing down upon the freshly-mown meadows and poppy-speckled fields of wheat, the stillness would be disturbed only by the sound of the local train which came rattling along the track at 7.50 every evening from the direction of Brambledown. The sound of a solitary door slamming shut might drift upwards from the scene spread out below, but there was little else to be heard. Moments later, it lazily drifted away from the station and disappeared behind the trees, its presence marked only by the dissipating tell-tale trail of steam. It's reappearance coincided with a resounding clatter of wheels over worn rail joints and the regular clanking of the engine's coupling rods, gradually dying away upon evening's cooling breeze which rustled the rippling sea of ripening corn. Here, on special occasions, the setting sun would suddenly break out from a gap within the purplish-leaden bank of western skyscape over London, its blazing reddish-amber brilliance turning the silvery snaking waters of the Swale to a shimmering orange fire. Such a brief and precious spectacle eventually made way for the cold, grey shadows of dusk which fingered their way across this tiny kingdom as the era of the old order came to an end.

The customary discomforts of war gradually began to make themselves apparent. In Sheppey, as elsewhere, there were disincentives and restrictions on travel, shortages of commodities, price rises, blackout regulations, as well as general economic and social depression. Gone were the days of the attractively-painted railway engines on the Leysdown branch, with their bright red coupling rods. Instead, those that now clanked along the winding track appeared on their rosters in the drab wartime grey livery whilst those on board peered from grimy steamed-up windows at the dreary, rain-sodden fields of wintertime gloom.

News of the casualties suffered filtered through with depressing regularity and there can have been few men employed on the SE & CR who didn't know someone who'd volunteered for military service and had 'copped it'. Chillingly, each week every provincial paper in the land published long lists of names of local men who'd fled into hiding and whose whereabouts were being sought for military conscription. Dim, dark wicked days where enthusiasm for 'settling once and for all the avaricious Hun' had long-since waned as deprivation and eventually epidemics stalked the country.

In this dismal atmosphere it isn't surprising that the island soon lost its electric tramway system. The war merely aggravated its poor financial and physical condition, in much the same way as the horse-drawn Hythe and Sandgate tramway on the south coast. Sheerness was therefore bestowed with the unenviable record of having the shortest-lived electric tramway in Great Britain. The motor 'buses, which the tram operators themselves

THE SHEPPEY LIGHT RAILWAY

In this glimpse of Minster, taken shortly before the Great War, a solid-tyred omnibus grinds its way along the rough roads of the district, quite probably robbing the railway of patrons.
Collection R. L. Ratcliffe

had purchased in 1914, only hastened the end. However, worst of all was the effect the new 'buses began to have on the Sheppey Light Railway. Whereas the trams were prevented from venturing further eastwards than Sheerness East station, the 'buses weren't hampered by such restrictions and were soon coaxing the public away. The railway was unable to compete with such door-to-door convenience, even if it hadn't been pre-occupied with the war effort. Thus, the seeds were being sown which would eventually reap a bitter harvest for those who relied on the local train service.

During the last days of the tramway the cars became rather shabby, the track remained unrepaired, whilst the effects of atrocious weather only compounded matters. It is also evident that the trams were viewed as a nuisance, an unfair charge since they could hardly be blamed for the public's disregard for safety in crossing the street, other road-users' ignorant behaviour and, worst of all, motorists' arrogant assumptions that they had sole right to the highways. Sadly, Mother Nature hadn't helped much at that time either. During the New Year of 1915, a 'terrific gale' had caused widespread damage to the tramway depot and cooling tower at Sheerness East. A smaller consequence of the storm involved a set of telephone wires being dislodged in Mile Town High Street with spectacular results. Late on that particular Monday evening, a tram had been ambling along when a 'sudden violent hissing and a flare of brilliant bright light' startled passengers on board. Yards of wire were trailed in the roadway, which caused onlookers to fear that someone had been electrocuted. However, a few soldiers on board put matters right by winding up what was realized to be telephone wire and not the overhead feeder.

The trams remained in operation for a further two seasons, but by the late spring of 1917 it was suddenly announced that the system was to 'close down immediately'. The company promptly offered the whole business to the council who, not surprisingly, declined. Most councillors expressed their regret, one of whom stated: 'the death knell was sounded when trams could go no further than Sheerness East station. If they'd been able to extend the line to Minster and so on, things would have been different'. Even though the tramway was prevented from fulfilling Mr Ramuz's cherished dream of reaching his grand Minster-on-Sea estate, as well as completing the anticipated Queenborough loop, it was the 'buses which sealed its fate. Whereas the tramway and the light railway had, in many senses, assisted one another with local passenger traffic, the 'buses plying along the Halfway House Road would do precisely the opposite. Their passengers remained firmly on board, continuing to Minster, Eastchurch and eventually Leysdown, robbing the railway of valuable custom and livelihood.

With the SE & CR coming under the control of the government during the war, numerous sidings and light railways were laid out to facilitate the movement and storage of supplies. Towards the end of 1916 engineers arrived at Eastchurch station where work had begun on laying down a siding leading into the Royal Naval Aviation School. Some months later the arrangements were ready for Col. Pringle from the Board of Trade to inspect and his report reads as follows:

'I have the honour to report for the information of the Board of Trade, that in compliance with the instructions contained in your minute of the 12th December 1916, I made an inspection of the new works at Eastchurch station on the South Eastern & Chatham Railway.

'A new siding for Admiralty purposes has been laid south of the railway at the Queenborough end of the station. The points on the single line are worked from an old groundframe "A" which contains 5 working and 1 spare lever. The points have an economical facing point lock, and an entrance ground signal for the siding has been provided. The interlocking in the frame is correct.

'The general arrangements of the station yard are not very satisfactory. The loop points are now worked by separate ground frames and the distance apart of these frames results in irregularity of signal working. I also observed that the goods loop – which, I understand, is not used for passenger services – is not equipped with catch points at either end. I inspected the Sheppey Light Railway in the year 1901, but can find no reason for the omission of catch points other than the possibility that the loop was intended for use by passenger trains. The working of the station yard should be controlled by a single ground frame, centrally situated. This would obviate irregularities in signal working which, I understand, now exist.

'Subject to the consideration of these matters at no distant date and to some satisfactory conclusion by the Committee, I recommend the Board of Trade to approve the new works.
'I have the honour etc.
J.W. Pringle, Colonel.'

It is evident that the SE & CR were not expecting the new works to be subjected to these preconditions, which would require greater expense, albeit borne by the Admiralty, as well as a delay in using the siding. Therefore, special permission had to be sought two days later as revealed by a telegram from the SE & CR to the BoT:

'3.24pm 21–7–17: REQUIRED TO USE ROYAL NAVAL AIR SERVICE SIDING AT EASTCHURCH FOR TRAINS CONVEYING CONSTRUCTION MATERIAL. SIDING NOT PASSED FOR TRAFFIC. SANCTION REQUIRED BEFORE SE & CRLY WILL PUT IN TRAIN AT PRESENT UNDER LOAD – URGENT.'

In the meantime, the SE & CR secretary, Francis Dent, wrote to the BoT assuring them that the new alterations required would be put in hand as soon as possible. Nevertheless, it wasn't until nine months later that the work, costing £208, was entirely completed to the BoT's satisfaction. However, a single, central, ground frame was not installed as recommended by Col. Pringle. Instead, both frames remained and this arrangement lasted until 1930.

It isn't surprising that the military establishments at Eastchurch should have attracted the attention of the enemy during the Great War. However, the Sheppey Light Railway is understood to have been bombed only once during the conflict. This happened on 29th September 1917 when a pot-shot, presumably aimed at Sheerness Dockyards, missed the mark and landed instead upon the railway. It scored a direct hit on the track some 300 yards on the Leysdown side of Sheerness East station, where

Taken around 1920, this postcard shows the guard house at the entrance to Eastchurch aerodrome which stood just beyond the level crossing.
Collection Martin Hawkins

Station Road, Eastchurch, showing the level crossing (by the farthest tree) in the days before gates were provided. The original signal is mostly obscured by the same tree.
Collection Martin Hawkins

This aerial view of Eastchurch aerodrome includes the Sheppey Light Railway which passes across the top of the picture. Of equal interest is the RNAS siding which can be seen leaving the goods yard and running parallel with the road, before curving into the depot.
Collection R. L. Ratcliffe

A panorama of the aerodrome taken from the railway, close to the level crossing.

Collection Richard Cullen

This view shows the goods sidings at Eastchurch station, as well as the RNAS siding, protected by a gate and running between the buildings seen on the left of the picture.

Collection Martin Hawkins

SHEPPEY LIGHT RAILWAY.—(One Class only.)

Down Trains— WEEK DAYS.

	a.m.	a.m.	a.m.	p.m.	p.m.	p.m.	Sats. only p.m.		SUNDAYS and Good Friday.		
									a.m.	p.m.	p.m.
Queenborough .... dep.	6 45	8 25	11 17	2 35	4 8	6 43	9 45		11 45	6 25	9 55
Sheerness East .... ,,	6 51	8 30	11 22	2 40	4 15	6 48	9 50		11 50	6 30	10 1
East Minster-on-Sea ...... ,,	6 55	8 34	11 26	2 44	4 20	6 52	9 54		11 54	6 35	10 5
Minster-on-Sea .... ,,	7 1	8 37	11 29	2 47	4 23	6 55	9 57		11 57	6 38	10 9
Brambledown Halt .... ,,	7 5	8 41	11 33	2 51	4 27	6 59	10 1		12 1	6 42	10 13
Eastchurch .... ,,	7 15	8 47	11 39	2 57	4 33	7 8	10 7		12 7	6 48	10 21
Harty Road Halt .... ,,	7 20	8 52	11 44	3 2	4 39	7 13	10 12		12 12	6 54	10 27
Leysdown .... arr.	7 25	8 57	11 49	3 7	4 44	7 18	10 17		12 17	6 59	10 32

Up Trains— WEEK DAYS.

	a.m.	a.m.	noon	p.m.	p.m.	p.m.	Sats. only p.m.		SUNDAYS and Good Friday.		
									p.m.	p.m.	p.m.
Leysdown .... dep.	7 33	9 3	12 0	3 15	5 25	7 40	10 25		12 35	7 8	10 40
Harty Road Halt .... ,,	7 38	9 8	12 5	3 20	5 30	7 46	10 30		12 40	7 13	10 45
Eastchurch .... ,,	7 43	9 13	12 10	3 27	5 40	7 53	10 35		12 45	7 19	10 50
Brambledown Halt .... ,,	7 49	9 19	12 16	3 33	5 46	7 59	10 41		12 51	7 25	10 56
Minster-on-Sea .... ,,	7 53	9 23	12 20	3 38	5 52	8 3	10 45		12 55	7 30	11 0
East Minster-on-Sea ...... ,,	7 56	9 26	12 23	3 41	5 55	8 7	10 48		12 58	7 35	11 3
Sheerness East .... ,,	8 0	9 30	12 27	3 45	6 1	8 11	10 52		1 2	7 39	11 7
Queenborough ..... arr.	8 5	9 35	12 32	3 50	6 6	8 16	10 57		1 7	7 44	11 12

Passenger timetable for 1916.

SHEPPEY LIGHT RAILWAY.

Down Trains—WEEK DAYS.

Dist. M. C.			p.m. arr.	p.m. dep				
.	Queenboro' ⎫			4 30				
1 40	Sheerness East		4 35	4 55				
2 44	East Minster-on-Sea		4 58	5 2				
3 10	Minster-on-Sea	A	5 5	5 25				
3 79	Brambledown Halt		5 29	5 31				
4 73	*Grove Siding*							
5 47	Eastchurch		5 33	5 43				
7 7	Harty Road Halt		5 49	5 51				
8 52	**Leysdown** ⎭		5 55					

Up Trains—WEEK DAYS.

Dist. M. C.			p.m. arr.	dep	Q p.m. arr.	dep
.	Leysdown ⎫			6 10		
1 45	Harty Road Halt		6 14	6 24		
2 0	*Holford Siding*		6 27	6 37		
3 5	Eastchurch		6 39	7 0	6 39	7 55
4 53	Brambledown Halt	A	7 5	7 8	8 5	8 15
5 42	Minster-on-Sea		7 12		8 18	8 35
6 8	East Minster-on-Sea		7 15	7 18	8 38	8 40
7 12	Sheerness East		7 22	7 27	8 43	8 53
8 52	**Queenboro'** ⎭		7 31		8 58	

—See Notes.

Instructions.—No Engine, Carriage, Wagon or other Vehicle (whether Loaded or Empty) the weight of which exceeds **14 Tons** on any pair of wheels must be used on this Light Railway, with the exception of the Ballast Engine now in use.

Speed must be reduced at all Level Crossings and Sharp Curves to **10** miles per hour. At the Accommodation or Farm Crossings, where no Gates are provided, Cattle Guards are put down. At all such Level Crossings where Gates are not erected and maintained across the Railway, the speed must be reduced to **10** miles an hour **for the distance of 300 yards approaching the Crossing.** Enginemen must sound the Whistle when approaching **all** Crossings.

In addition to Public Road Crossings, numerous Farm and Accommodation Crossings exist, some of which are provided with Gates, and others with Cattle Guards, but no Gates.

Minster Station on this Railway must always be referred to as **Minster-on-Sea** in all entries *re* Goods, etc., as a distinction from Minster Junction **(Thanet).**

Freight timetable for 1916.

Drove Road crossed the line. The blast blew out the rails, sending large fragments of metal skywards which then fell into the fields of Danley Farm. Immediate repairs were put in hand and by the following day the line was back in operation.

Throughout the war the service of passenger trains averaged six trips each way, with an augmented late run on Wednesdays and Saturdays. On Sundays there were just two trains each way, one around midday, the other early in the evening. For passenger working during this period, the SE & CR used set No. 40 which comprised three third class vestibuled saloons and one third class six-wheeled carriage with a brake compartment. Motive power appears to have been provided by 'O' class engines which also handled the goods services. Don Bradley's father, who likewise took a great interest in railways, was based at Sheerness in 1915-16 and took the opportunity to travel over the local lines and make notes. He made four trips upon the light railway, in October 1915 and January, April and July of 1916. On all occasions he found the passenger services being worked with Stirling's 'O' class and noted down Nos. 8, 333, 382 and 100. Don Bradley surmised that this was probably on account of the extra supplies being run to the RNAS base at Eastchurch since the working timetable of that period indicates daily trains of petrol, aero engines and foodstuffs. Freight workings are shown in the accompanying timetable.

Following the armistice and the return to more civilised times, many Sheppeyites must have wondered what the future held for the 'Holiday Isle'. It was almost a different world which emerged from the ashes of the old. Many people's spirits had been exhausted by the emerging futility of the war, whilst hearts grieved for those who'd perished in the shattered meadows of France and Belgium. Feelings of resentment helped crumble many of the old social structures of class and custom, whilst this in turn had a direct effect upon the resorts and business on the railways. Part of this change, as well as the demand for better wages by ordinary folk, led to more people finding they were able to afford days out at the seaside. This especially benefited all the resorts along both sides of the Thames Estuary, and Sheppey soon regained its popularity. Year by year, the day-trippers and holidaymakers increased, the SE & CR responding with a train service to Leysdown of six trips each way, augmented to seven on Saturdays. On Sundays there were four in summer, but only two in winter. At the height of the season the demand sometimes required a relief train being organised, whilst on the roads there were charabanc trips conveying parties of windswept

Londoners to the island. These often had to queue at the King's Ferry toll bridge as with each season the lines of waiting road vehicles increased.

A major upset affected the island and in December 1922 when the SS *Gyp* collided with the King's Ferry bridge. A makeshift ferry transported people and supplies across the Swale, whilst the SE & CR arranged temporary working up to both sides of the river crossing for the duration. A ferry was also introduced between Sheerness, Queenborough and Port Victoria with the aid of the paddle steamer *Princess of Wales*. Because of the lack of motive power on the island when the bridge was breached, it is recorded that a Peckett 0–6–0 saddle tank, belonging to Messrs. Settle Speakman, was borrowed from their Queenborough coal wharves to run a skeleton service over the Leysdown branch.

It was originally hoped to have the bridge operational once more by the following October, but postwar delays in obtaining suitable materials postponed the re-opening. Nonetheless, a sigh of relief went up when, after almost a full year, normal working over the only road and rail access to the island was resumed. However, the reintroduction of tolls caused widespread dismay, a bone of contention that lasted for several more years.

Following the grouping, the emergent Southern Railway Company took charge of an expansive system stretching the breadth of southern England. Understandably, the status of a light railway running out to a largely undeveloped seaside hamlet on the Thames Estuary diminished somewhat. Leysdown suffered the added disadvantage of having no through trains, as well as being at the end of a rather long and circuitous journey via Chatham, Sittingbourne and Queenborough. This normally involved three separate train journeys, so a determined effort to reach the little resort had to be made by those from south London.

In spite of these drawbacks, the SR turned its attention to the carriage stock employed on the branch. The quaint, but rather musty vehicles, which dated from the days of Queen Victoria's reign, had seen far better times and it was plainly apparent that they wouldn't encourage people to patronise the company's trains. Suitable replacements came from a most unusual source when someone suggested using the old railmotors. The Southern had received all eight of the redundant machines in 1923. These had been lying derelict for a number of years, some in the sidings at Crystal Palace (High Level), while others had been deteriorating on the closed branch line to Greenwich Park. They were clearly useless for returning to traffic in their original form, so the diminutive locomotives and carriage portions were separated from each other. All but one of the engines went for immediate scrap, whilst the saloons were cleverly converted for re-use. Those from Nos. 1, 2, 3 and 8 were paired up to form two articulated sets, becoming set No. 514 and 513 respectively. Following a thorough overhaul and the application of the smart

Still in its austere wartime livery, a 'Q' class 0–4–4T, No. 73, crossing the flat marshland between Queenborough and Sheerness East with the 11.17 a.m. service to Leysdown on 22nd October 1921.
Ken Nunn/LCGB

Southern Railway livery, they were sent to the island and were distinguished by being the only articulated stock owned by the SR. It is doubtful whether any of the islanders recognised them in their new guise, since these former 'boneshakers' now ran smoothly and comfortably, hauled as conventional stock.

Around this time the 'P' class locomotives made a brief return visit to the island when Nos. 325 and 558 were sent to Sheerness for working the light railway. During the early part of 1923 they had both been sent to Ashford works to prepare them for motor-train working. They proved to be a dismal failure and were soon returned to the mainland where more suitable tasks might be found. No. 558 then went off to the West Country, being sent as far as Cornwall for trial trips over the Wenford Bridge china clay line.

Although precise details are not known, it is thought to have been only during the war and up until the mid-1920s that the 'Q' class 0–4–4 tank locomotives were seen on the light railway. In his book on the locomotives of the SER, Don Bradley relates that No. 73 was stationed there up until 1922 when it was required to leave the rural, breezy line for duties in the smog-bound districts of south London. Its place was taken by an elderly 'O' class, No. 99, which found its second breath plying at a leisurely pace along the undulating branch in its last few years of active life. Other 'Q' class engines known to have worked the line were Nos. 23 and A72 which Don's father noted on his two visits in April 1921 and May 1925 respectively. In a letter, Don Bradley stated: 'I believe all these engines were only on loan to the area for from 1914 the SE & CR Allocation List only ever refers to:-

'An "O" to work line/or a "Q" to work line, exchange to be arranged by Bricklayers Arms each Sunday.'

He continues: 'The SE & CR working timetables of 1912–5 and 1918 all give 14 tons maximum axle loading (which permits the "O"s) whilst the Southern Railway 1924 Rule Book raises this to $15\frac{1}{2}$ tons which covers the "O1" class and the "Q"s (after the weight re-arrangement of 1919–22)'. Don Bradley also mentioned that the ballast engine on Sheppey in 1916–18 was ex-LC & DR 'B1' 0-6-0 No. 612, although 'B2' 0-6-0 No. 656 was there in July 1916. Eventually, though, the SR was able to send down the ex-LC & DR 'R' and 'R1' class 0-4-4Ts, displaced by suburban electrification in the mid-20s. These proved perfect for the job and formed the mainstay of the motive power throughout the rest of the line's existence.

Life for the islanders continued to settle down following the deprivation and hardship of the war, but times were still bleak for some. In February 1925 a thief broke into the booking office at Minster-on-Sea station by forcing open the window on the platform side. The miscreant made away with £1 7s 6d, which at that time was about two-thirds of a week's wages for a signalman. Pilfering was always rife and not so lucky was one chap who, in 1908, had been stopped in Station Road, Minster, by a suspicious constable. Concealed within a rough hessian sack he was found carrying away 'three-quarters of a hundredweight of old iron belonging to the SE & C Railway Company'. It was reckoned to be worth only 1s 9d, but it does illustrate the extraordinary lengths to which some individuals were prepared to go in order to gain an extra 'bob' or two.

Come the middle of the decade the pace of change in social habits had quickened and, not surprisingly, the SR felt the need to re-assess its system and make adjustments accordingly. Lesser-used lines were subsequently scrutinised to see where economies might be effected. Public road vehicles were becoming ever more popular, not only the privately-hired charabancs, but also the local 'bus which ran to a schedule in direct competition with many branch railway lines. Rather than set about beating the opposition, the SR began taking up shares in the new companies which were mostly amalgamations of the smaller concerns. The Sheppey Light Railway, in common with all the other rural lines, started to lose business to the road operators who vied for the same passengers, rather than performing a public service by complementing the trains. Evidence of the alarming degree of this drift onto the roads is revealed in a census taken on the Leysdown Road during the week 9th-15th August 1926 in comparison with an identical count in 1923. It registered a staggering three-fold increase over the three year period. During the week in 1926 the following vehicles were logged:

'R' class 0-4-4T No. A674 pulling into East Minster-on-Sea with a train from Leysdown, comprising the articulated stock, during the late 1920s.
Collection Roger Carpenter

```
1,978 motor cars
1,741 motor cycles
  190 'buses
  223 vans
   98 lorries
2,607 bicycles
```

These tallies speak for themselves and the loss felt by the railway may easily be imagined simply by bearing in mind the absence of available alternatives before the Great War.

The wintertime Sunday service was the first casualty and this was soon followed by the suspension of the summer Sunday trains. However, this move was greeted with so many protests from holiday-makers and the councils that the SR was obliged to acquiesce and restore the service. Even so, the Sunday trains ran only for three months during July, August and September.

At the beginning of 1930 a fairly major alteration was made in the method of working the branch, with simultaneous modifications to the signalling. This took place over the weekend of 18th/19th January. The SR had decided to introduce the availability of 'Long Section Staff' working which would enable them to make certain economies, most notably in manpower employed at Leysdown and Eastchurch. The precise details of the revision are reproduced in the appendix, but in simple terms it allowed the line to be worked under the 'one engine in steam' principle, whenever required, and without the need to issue train staff tickets. Concurrently, ground frame 'B' at Eastchurch was abolished, whereby its signal and point movements were transferred to 'A' frame at the Queenborough end of the station. It is surmised that, in all probability, the wooden cabin built around ground frame 'A' was put up at this time. At Leysdown the up starting and down home signals were removed, although the post of the latter was retained to carry a yellow location light for the benefit of the train crews.

The early days of the Sheppey Light Railway were recalled in the local newspaper when, in 1932, it reported the retirement of Henry Walkling, chief inspector at Chatham. He recalled that he'd entered the service of the LC & DR in 1891 as a junior porter at Southfleet station on the Gravesend West branch. 'Those were the days when we did work' he claimed, adding that they started at the time when the first train left in the morning and didn't go home until the last one had departed. 'There was no eight hour day, whilst Sundays were treated like any other day – and all for fifteen and eight [15s 8d] a week!' he exclaimed. One of his most vivid memories was during the period when the SE & CR took official control of the Sheppey Light Railway. He was rostered to be the guard on the first 'big train' – a rake of six coaches which were run from Queenborough to Leysdown. He recalled that it was a very rough ride indeed as the 'road' was, to put it mildly, 'a bit shaky'. However, he remarked that once the SE & CR had strengthened the bed of the permanent way, matters improved markedly and the line was able to stand much heavier traffic.

Even though the motor 'buses of the Maidstone & District Company were stealing the bulk of the line's former passenger traffic, a healthy business in freight prevented the railway from being closed in a period of contraction during the 'thirties. With the Southern Railway having more than a finger in many a 'bus company's pie, it was perhaps indeed fortunate for the islanders that the agricultural trade ensured the line's retention as part of the system. From the available evidence, Leysdown seems to have clung on to a fair proportion of the holidaymaker traffic, although nothing near what it once enjoyed. Eastchurch was considerably cushioned from what could so easily have been a tough time by the comings and goings of airmen at the nearby aerodrome. The Royal Air Force, as it had now become, obviously found the base useful, whilst the 'boys' as they were known, were familiar friends with all the villagers and even more so with the local girls! One of their favourite haunts was 'The Ritz', – not a palatial hotel that had sprung up in Eastchurch, but their cheeky nickname for the Station Tea Rooms adjacent to the level crossing.

Eastchurch residents were well used to seeing the uniformed officers and men around the village, as well as the aeroplanes which took off and landed a mile or so away. However, there was some considerable excitement in September 1932 when an unexpected visitor suddenly appeared out of the sky. This was the 'giant German air liner', the *Luft-Hansa* which, it was stated, passed over Sheppey every day on its trips between Amsterdam and Croydon. Owing to the especially bad weather, the pilot was obliged to make a forced landing at Eastchurch. By the next morning it was able to resume its journey, its German pilot having been guest of the officers at the RAF station, whilst the crew and passengers spent the night up in the village at the 'Crooked Billet'.

With the increase in traffic upon the island's primitive roads, it followed that the incidents of collisions at the open level crossings began to increase. A serious accident occurred in January 1929 at Scraps Gate Crossing, between Sheerness East and East Minster-on-Sea stations. Even though gates were provided at this site, they opened outwards and were secured by bolts to the roadside. The crossing wasn't manned, but all trains were required to approach at 10 mph, with the whistle being sounded. At about 9.25am the nine o'clock service from Leysdown was on its way to Queenborough, the driver having blown his engine's whistle on leaving East Minster and again just before the crossing. As he approached Scraps Gate he noticed a lorry coming down the road which appeared to be racing the train. This lorry, which belonged to Messrs Clay & Sons, was loaded with asbestos roofing tiles and to the train crew's disbelief it simply ran straight onto the crossing whereupon it received a sharp blow from the locomotive's buffers. The force of the impact was so great that it wrenched the steering wheel from out of the lorry driver's hands, pushed the vehicle aside and threw its occupant into the ditch. Having pulled up their train, the crew hurriedly attended to the young chap who had sustained cuts about the head, neck and hands. In the meantime a gang of platelayers working nearby ran down the track and assisted in dragging away the wreckage which had broken fencing and had scratched the paintwork of the articulated carriage set from end to end. After recovering from shock, the lorry driver was able to walk down the lane to the doctor's surgery in Minster Road, whilst the train continued its journey. No blame was attributed to the engine crew who had acted properly. Instead, the fault was deemed that of the irresponsible lorry driver who had foolishly attempted to beat the train.

Apart from collisions with road vehicles, there were sporadic incidents involving livestock, as well as other mishaps as might be expected on this rural, windswept line. In mid-May, that same year, the 10.45am Queenborough-Leysdown service was approaching Stickfast Lane Crossing, between Minster-on-Sea and Brambledown Halt, when the driver observed a number of lambs on the line as his train rounded a curve. Speed was quickly reduced and by the time they were reached the animals were well clear of the track. However, in the general panic, two lambs were killed when they suddenly darted between the engine and leading coach.

Broken fences were sometimes to blame for these incidents, but usually it was careless farm hands or members of the public who left gates open. Two bullocks were killed because of this in August 1930 at Frog's Island Crossing near Harty Road by the 6.45am train to Leysdown. Eighteen months later, at the same crossing, Mr G. Love of Pump Farm had to have one of his prize bullocks destroyed after it was seriously injured by the evening train out of Leysdown. The force of the impact was so great that the leading step on the engine was broken. Although there were no gates at the crossing, the animal had wandered onto the track through a field gate being thoughtlessly left open.

Occasionally, accidents were simply caused by quirks of fate or the effects of bad weather. This was the case in January 1929 when, in pitch darkness, the 10.28pm to Leysdown ran through the first crossing gate at East Minster-on-Sea. It was a wild, dark and stormy night as the late [Wednesdays and Saturdays-only] service made its way across the island. Since it was the custom for the guard on the train to open the gates, the driver approached with caution. Both gates had red lamps, which had been observed alight on the previous trip from Leysdown, but the howling wind had obviously extinguished the nearest one to the train. As a result, the driver mistook his distance and promptly reduced the barrier to matchwood.

On that occasion the driver was found blameless, but not quite so fortunate were three railwaymen at Queenborough, a

The loss of the tramway was much regretted by many Sheppey folk who either had to walk or take to their bicycles — somehow the 'buses were never quite the same. On a hot, drowsy afternoon in the 1920s people of all ages stroll around the empty road, bereft of tramlines and overhead wires and in the days before cars cluttered our streets. *Author's collection*

signalman, shunter and driver, who made rather a mess of the shunting in February 1933. They were busy with the 1.0am freight train from Bricklayers Arms when, at a quarter to six in the morning, the engine with three wagons attached at the London end and one at the Sheerness end, set off over No.14 points to the 'up' siding and promptly derailed two of its wagons. This not only blocked the line to Sheerness, but also access to the Sheppey Light. The Faversham breakdown crane was duly summoned, arriving at 7.17am, but it took two hours to clear both lines, during which a 'bus service had to be organised for the 6.44am and 8.16am Leysdown trips. All three railwaymen involved were subsequently cautioned for their careless actions.

Curiously enough, perhaps, the same set of points was responsible for a derailment almost two years to the day in 1935. On this dark, cold morning, 'R1' class No.1697 had been giving assistance to the 3.25am freight from Faversham to Sheerness Dockyard. Having completed its task, the locomotive came off and ran back light to Queenborough to take on water in readiness for working the early morning service to Leysdown. Finding themselves 'off the road', the steam crane from Bricklayers Arms was sent for and this arrived at eight o'clock. It took two and a half hours before 1697 was back on the rails, the line eventually being cleared at 11.07am. Throughout the period 'buses replaced trains, but this time the incident was put down to an 'error of misunderstanding'.

Following the serious accident with the lorry at Scraps Gate, the SR altered these gates so that their normal position should be across the railway. Perhaps the driver of the 4.15pm freight from Queenborough forgot about this, for on the afternoon of 4th May 1933 his sudden application of the brakes couldn't prevent his train sliding into and wrecking the first gate. For this mishap the driver involved was subsequently reprimanded.

In the light of the recent spate of accidents at the ungated level crossings, the superintendent of operation reviewed the current arrangements concerning the sounding of engine whistles, suggesting they should be held open continuously from the whistle boards until the crossing was reached. In the majority of cases this was already the practice at distances of 300, 200 and 100 yards according to the positions of boards, but there were anomalies. Two lines stood out as oddities, the Sheppey Light and the Bordon branch in Hampshire. Falling into this category were: Minster Road (at Minster-on-Sea station); Stickfast Lane (between Minster-on-Sea and Brambledown); Newhook Farm (between Brambledown and Eastchurch); Mustards Road and Frog's Island (between Harty Road and Leysdown). 'Beware of Trains' notices were affixed on the roadside verges, whilst all trains were required to reduce speed to ten miles an hour, with the whistle sounded momentarily only at the approach. The superintendent was uneasy over this, citing the example of the Bere Alston and Callington branch in Devon, where there were crossings of similar character. Here, the crews were instructed to sound their whistles continuously from the board to the roadway. He considered a similar arrangement should be adopted on the Sheppey Light. However, the London East Division Superintendent disagreed and wrote on 9th April 1935 to say:

'Level crossings without gates:

Referring to your letter of the 29th ultimo: I have given this matter consideration and am of opinion that the present arrangements operating on the Sheppey Light Line are satisfactory for that branch and recommend that no change be made.

To increase the whistling would be against the principle recently reviewed in connection with the question of Zones of Silence – Engine Whistling, and may lead to complaints from residents near the Crossings concerned.'

Fate was indeed to prove it had a cruel sense of timing, for it was surely ironic that only seventeen days after this letter was written there occurred one of the most serious accidents on the line. It is also open to conjecture that had the ruling been changed during that fortnight the tragedy might possibly have been averted.

The occasion was a pleasant evening in late spring when, on Friday 26th April, a car was running along the winding lanes from Minster on its way to Queenborough, its four occupants intent on going to the cinema there. Driving the car was Mrs Marshall, accompanied by her husband, with a young couple in the back seat. It was about ten past seven when they came gliding down Station Road at Minster, at the same time that the 6.55pm from Queenborough was approaching. Within a matter of seconds it was all over as the car collided with the locomotive, its offside completely wrecked. The young man was killed, whilst the other three were badly injured.

At the subsequent enquiry held by the Ministry of Transport on 8th May, evidence was given by numerous witnesses to establish the cause of the accident. Engine driver Frank Walden stated that his train (comprising articulated set No.513 and 'R1' No.1696), had been travelling at 15 mph after leaving East Minster-on-Sea, speed being reduced on passing the 10 mph board. He had given a long blast on the whistle as he'd seen some children playing on the crossing up ahead. On the approach, speed was further reduced to 7 mph when, in a flash, he saw the car dart from behind the hedge and hit his engine. There was nothing he could have done to prevent the collision.

Visibility at the crossing was not very good, although railwaymen considered it to be one of the safest on the branch. However, over the years the hedges bordering the road had been neglected and warning notices were difficult to see. There was only a cast iron 'Beware of Trains' notice in either direction, painted black letters on white, but it was remarked that even these needed a fresh coat of paint. Due to accidents and calls for improved safety, gates had been provided at Scraps Gate and at Eastchurch station, but apparently no one considered Minster to be dangerous.

Enquiring into the method of operation, the SR stated that there was a porter in attendance for most of the day and it was his duty to flag the trains across. However, since the accident occurred outside his hours of duty, they admitted there would have been no one in attendance. At this, the solicitor appearing for Mrs Marshall retorted: 'It boils down to this. Rather than a man should be employed and given a week's wages, the public has to take it's chance?'. 'To a certain extent' was the reply he was given.

A heavily-bandaged Mrs Marshall then gave her account, although she admitted she couldn't remember much about the accident, it happened so quickly. She remarked that it was common knowledge among the villagers that there was a man with a flag standing in the roadway whenever a train was due. In consequence, she'd not expected to see a train.

Porter Brown was then called and he was able to brief the enquiry on his duties in which he always signalled every train over the crossing using a green flag. To warn any approaching road vehicles he would hold up his hand, much like a policeman on traffic duty. Most road users obeyed his instructions but, he added, motor cycles frequently slipped through.

A young lad, 7 year old Harry Barnes, who lived near the line, then came forward to say that he had been one of the children playing on the crossing and had gone to stand by the station entrance gate when he heard the engine whistling. He looked round and saw a car coming down Station Road. 'I got into the middle of the road and put my hand out to warn the car, but it didn't slow down and was travelling fast'. This corroborated with the engine driver's remark that the car was moving at no less than thirty miles an hour. The fact that the car, an Austin 7, had struck the leading wheel of the locomotive and had been so badly damaged before being thrown aside certainly gave weight to this view.

In reviewing the practice adopted at this particular open crossing, the engine driver revealed that he'd worked the branch for over 30 years and it was the custom for trains to be flagged. At one time, he remarked, the service included several through trains which didn't stop at Minster-on-Sea, so he thought flagging had been introduced to aid safety.

The guard on the train, Bertie Wyatt, then came forward as he'd been looking out and witnessed the car strike the engine. He said he'd never received any complaint about that particular crossing, nor heard of any accident there. 'But', he added indignantly, 'I have seen other instances where motorists have treated us with contempt; a sort of "Harry Tate's" railway! They have dashed across the road ahead of us, at the risk of their necks, as you might put it. There have been narrow escapes, but they have merely sneered at us and treated it as a joke'.

A verdict of 'Accidental Death' was recorded by the jury since it was agreed that blame could not be laid on any individual. In summing up for the MoT, Lt. Col. E. Woodhouse recommended that Kent County Council should erect notices along the roadside; that the hedges should be properly maintained; and that the SR should either provide staff to flag every train, or else erect gates. The latter directive was subsequently adopted.

There was also much correspondence between the various departments at that time concerning the irregular positions of the whistle and speed restriction boards which protected the numerous crossings. Attention was drawn to the fact that there appeared to be no whistle board applying to trains from Queenborough approaching Newhook crossing. The chief engineer pointed out that there was a 10 mph restriction and whistle sign some fifty yards on the down approach to Brambledown, which they concluded must have been put up before the SE & CR built the halt. It was assumed the engineers of the Sheppey Light Railway had intended this notice should serve for both the Lower Road crossing at Brambledown and Newhook. Delving further into the mystery, the chief engineer was able to establish from his records that 'a platform had been put up in the early part of 1905', whilst the shelter was erected during 1907. He also mentioned that old SE & CR timetables first showed the halt in use in May 1907.

Since all trains were required to stop at Brambledown level crossing in order to operate the gates, the locomotive running superintendent raised no objection to the resiting of the whistle board to a new position some ten yards on the Leysdown side of the crossing. This action, carried out in February 1936, complied with the original conditions laid down in the Light Railway Order that such speed restriction and relevant notices should be erected about 300 yards in both directions on all level crossings without gates.

The level crossing at Eastchurch was also the subject of current debate, although for entirely different reasons. One particular

in the platform he gives attention to it, exchanges the staff [single-line token] and then closes the gates across the roadway. If he closed the gates across the road before he lowered the Home signal, they would be closed 5 to 6 minutes, as it takes 2 minutes to walk from the Crossing to the ground frame, 2 minutes back and then there is attention to be given to the train. The distance from the Crossing to the ground frame is 200 yards.

After the train has departed, the man replaces the gates across the line and returns to the ground frame and replaces the Home signal to 'Danger'.

'R' class No. A697 simmering gently at Leysdown in charge of an afternoon service made up with an articulated set. This stock enjoyed a thorough overhaul and repaint not long afterwards.
H. A. Vallance

incident probably prompted matters to be reviewed, as related by a Sheppey resident, Mr Vic Martin of Warden. On this Boxing Day morning Mr Martin was walking back to Warden along the Harty Road when he heard the train from Leysdown approaching as he reached the level crossing. Intending to be helpful, he shut the gates across the roadway so the train might proceed, thus saving the crew the trouble of doing it themselves. On this day, a 'C' class was operating the service and running tender first on the journey back to Queenborough. The following day, Mr Martin had some business to attend to at Eastchurch station, but was surprised on his arrival to see the level crossing gates there had been smashed and were lying by the trackside. He learned that it had happened the previous day when a train 'running tender first' had apparently ignored them. Since the signals in both directions were always normally in the 'off' or clear position during the 'long staff' block operation, the crew had mistakenly assumed these gates were also open.

The driver and fireman were clearly to blame on this occasion, as illustrated in a letter from the LED Superintendent:

'It should be pointed out that when the long staff is in operation the signals must of necessity be off with the gates closed against the Railway, but when this working is in operation, the train crew attend to the gates and it is their responsibilty to stop before reaching them.'

He was also aware of the difficulties experienced there by the station porter who also had to act as signalman during the normal working. These were explained thus:

Trains from the Queenborough Direction:
The Porter, after accepting a train from Minster-on-Sea on the telephone in the Booking Office, goes to the ground frame and lowers the Home signal from Queenborough. When the train arrives

Trains from the Leysdown Direction:
With these trains also the Home signal from Leysdown is lowered before the gates are closed against the road.

In these cases the Porter closes the gates approximately 3 minutes before the train arrives. There is the fact, however, that the signal is 'off' with the gates across the Railway, and with the other duties to perform, it does sometimes happen that the man has difficulty in correctly gauging the three minute interval.

In order to overcome the expense of moving the ground frame, which is in a position convenient to the points of the Yard and also to the RAF siding, I would suggest that levers for each Home signal be provided in the office, so that the Porter can keep the signals to 'Danger' until the Crossing gates are across the road.

With regard to the trains from the Queenborough direction, I would suggest that the instruction with regard to the closing of the gates be altered to read 'One minute before the train is due to arrive', as all trains call at Eastchurch and to avoid a long hold-up of road traffic.

Numerous suggestions were put forward, including the replacement of the running signals with location indicators only. Alternatively, shunt signals could be provided showing either a red or amber aspect, otherwise a new 'down' starting signal would have to be erected at the Leysdown end of Eastchurch station.

It seems the main objection to the present system centred around the fact that trains from Leysdown, in hours of darkness, approached the crossing on a falling gradient with the crews being confronted by a green aspect on the signal and the gates across the running lines just a few yards ahead. A further difficulty involved a particular working each day where it was necessary to deal with one train at Eastchurch, while another train (goods) was in the sidings. It was suggested, therefore, that Eastchurch should be abolished as a passing place and that the goods engine could go through to Leysdown to work the following passenger service as well. P. Nunn, the LED Divisional Superintendent, was not in favour of doing this since the traffic at Eastchurch was increasing at that time. There had been a significant rise in the number of RAF personnel using the station, the RAF Depot having approximately a thousand men stationed there during 1936. It was also expected that special trains would have to be run. Neither was it feasible to re-time the services since the trains in question took schoolchildren home from Sittingbourne to Leysdown. He also revealed that there had been some further development on the island and that the SR was considering improving the service. Furthermore, special trains had been run during 1935 and if the goods train was re-timed then it would be impossible to find a path for the party specials.

Other complications were also brought to light, for example the platelayers would not be able to operate their motor trolley to Eastchurch if the whole line was operated as one section, i.e. Queenborough-Leysdown. There was also a valuable trade in sheep traffic during early April which could only be handled in daylight hours. It was noted that Mr Wright, the farmer who received and forwarded the sheep, had a contract worth £400 per annum with the SR. Finally, the passenger bookings were rising as a result of the presence of the RAF. Indeed, comparing the passenger takings at Eastchurch the figures speak for themselves:

April 1935: £47 18s 7d   May 1935: £30 13s 6d
April 1936: £122 18s 2d   May 1936: £62 4s 8d

The abolition of Eastchurch as a passing place was therefore deemed impractical, yet the SR was reluctant to spend over £150 on moving the 'up' Home signal to the other side of the gates or installing a ground frame within the station building. Mr Nunn said he would have no objection to the signal remaining where it was, so long as it only showed an amber aspect when 'off'. The matter appears to have subsequently been resolved with a simple instruction to enginemen:

Buying a ticket on the Sheppey Light Railway usually involved the guard on the train who would pass along the articulated set. The interior of the brake compartment is interesting, as is the rather striking moquette of the upholstery.   *H. F. Wheeller*

At Brambledown Halt the duty of opening and closing the gates also fell to the guard. Here, the small wooden gates are shut to enable 'C' class No. 1252 to proceed with the Leysdown train, probably causing little disruption to the meagre road traffic. *H. F. Wheeller*

SHEPPEY LIGHT RAILWAY.

The instructions under the above heading relating to level crossings on page 43, and those relating to Eastchurch Station level crossing on page 10 of No. 5 supplement, are superseded by the following :—

Level Crossings.—The signals at Eastchurch Station are not interlocked with the level crossing gates and during the period when the station staff are off duty the signals will be maintained in the " off " position with the level crossing gates across the railway. A similar situation may also arise during those periods when the staff are on duty at Eastchurch Station, and a Driver of a train approaching Eastchurch must be prepared at all times to bring the train to a stand clear of the level crossing gates.

The gates at Sheerness East, Scrapps Gate (between Sheerness East and East Minster), East Minster, Minster Road (Minster-on-Sea), Brambledown, Eastchurch and Harty Road level crossings are normally closed across the railway.

When a member of the Traffic department staff is on duty at Sheerness East, Minster-on-Sea and Eastchurch stations he will operate the level crossing gates. When no member of the Traffic department staff is on duty the level crossing gates must be operated by the trainmen as shown below :—

At Sheerness East and Minster Road (Minster-on-Sea) crossings the gates must be opened and closed by the Fireman, except that the duty of closing the gates after the passing of an up train must be performed by the Guard.

At Eastchurch the gates must be opened and closed by the Fireman, except that the duty of closing the gates after the passing of a down train must be performed by the Guard.

The gates at Scrapps Gate, East Minster, Brambledown and Harty Road level crossings must be operated by the Guard.

In the event of a light engine travelling over the line the gates in each case must (except when a member of the Traffic Department staff is on duty at the places previously specified) be operated by the Fireman.

Instructions issued to enginemen during 1936.

This view, shortly after arrival at Leysdown on 2nd June 1936, shows No. 1252 uncoupled and about to run round to the other end of its train. By this time the starting signal had been dispensed with, but water facilities remained out of necessity. In the foreground is the engine pit.
H. F. Wheeller

Mr. Card, porter at Leysdown, posing for the camera as locals and some boy scouts leave the train.
Collection Jeremy Segrove

This splendid broadside view of set No. 514 at Leysdown station shows the unit after its full repaint in SR livery. *H. F. Wheeller*

Motive power on the branch was now almost exclusively handled by the 'R's and 'R1's. From time to time, however, more unusual vistors were to be seen running across the lonely fields, pulling behind them the articulated set or the daily goods. In 1936 'C' class 0-6-0 No.1252 spent a brief spell here, but its appearance was probably not quite so remarkable as that of 'B1' No.1021, an elegant 4-4-0 and one of the last locomotives built in 1898 by James Stirling for the South Eastern Railway. Normally, though, it was the familiar and much-loved 'R1's which became the idol of every local boy who dreamed of growing up to be an engine driver.

In 1937 the Sheerness newspapers began campaigning for better railway facilities. They were of the opinion that most people exclaimed: 'Oh yes, Sheppey is very nice, but it takes so long to get there and I find I can get to Brighton and Southend in half the time'. Even so, the Southern Railway did its best to promote the resorts on the island:

A rare visitor to the line, 'C' class No. 1252, waiting at Leysdown with the return service on 2nd June 1936. *H. F. Wheeller*

'SHEPPEY – THE HOLIDAY ISLE:
The air is bracing and the scenery bright and interesting, the seascapes including innumerable vessels of all sizes and nationalities passing the coast to and from the Thames and Medway. There is much to attract the visitor, including fine cliff rambles and a number of picturesque villages, easily accessible by rail or by the Maidstone and District Company's 'buses. Enjoyable cliff and inland rambles over the Island may be taken and the light railway, also the 'buses of the Maidstone and District Omnibus Co., are available for longer journeys. There are daily steamer trips up the Medway, also to other resorts on the coast. The Naval activities at Sheerness are always a source of interest and visitors are heartily invited to view the new Museum within H.M. Dockyard, whilst the Government aerodrome at Eastchurch provides some very entertaining flying spectacles.'

In spite of these inducements and the fact that Sheerness was the same distance by rail from London as Brighton, the journeys were longer and less frequent. The only advantage was that ordinary fares to Sheerness were a shilling less than Brighton, but a cheap day return to Brighton, at 6s 10d, was only tenpence extra for the superior attractions on offer. The Isle of Sheppey also faced rivalry from the neighbouring 'resort' across the Medway where the Southern Railway had, in 1932, tried to create 'Allhallows-on-Sea'. For a brief period this infant enterprise promised to develop into a seaside suburb for weary Londoners, and with a spur line connected into the line to Port Victoria, the Southern hoped for greater things. Allhallows was able to boast the cheapest fares among the Southern's resorts and it certainly appealed to the hordes who flocked here in their hundreds to see what was on offer. Whereas Allhallows was just 37 miles away for 5s 3d, Leysdown was almost twenty miles further by rail. However, it tried its best to retain its share of the market:

'LEYSDOWN-ON-SEA:
56 miles from London, in the Isle of Sheppey, is a growing holiday and residential resort. An exceedingly healthy climate, low rainfall, glorious sands, and perfectly safe bathing (which is free, excepting when bathing huts are used, for which a charge of 6d is made), added to provision for all kinds of sports, including golf and tennis, make this an ideal rendezvous for permanent residence or holidays. An hotel, designed on Country Club lines, with Club licence and

The sense of independence lingered very strongly among the staff; even the legend 'Sheppey Light Railway' continued to be displayed on the carriage boards. *H. F. Wheeller*

The smart Maunsell livery applied by the SR may be appreciated in this close-up shot of the articulated section. *H. F. Wheeller*

commodious lounge, has been built on the beach, to augment the already ample accommodation for holiday makers, who are coming here in greater numbers year by year. Houses and bungalows being built are designed to enhance, rather than detract from the natural beauty of the village. An attractive dance hall adjoins the hotel, which is also used for theatrical entertainments, and is equipped with a cinema apparatus.'

Nearby Warden Bay is thus described:

'WARDEN BAY is a bungalow resort on a private estate which has been developed within the last few years, 1½ miles from Leysdown Station. The estate, being private, makes a special point of catering for the interests of those wishing for a quiet and peaceful holiday. The special attractions, apart from the splendidly healthy climate, include safe bathing, fine sands for children, and the picturesque brown soil cliffs, beautified by bush undergrowth, which make such admirable picnicking or sunbathing spots.'

Speculative developers attempted to persuade dwellers in suburbia to 'Live at Leysdown!'. However, like Allhallows, it seems it gradually became clear that the area would not develop in the fashion as had once been anticipated.

Two charming glimpses of Scraps Gate crossing between East Minster-on-Sea and Sheerness East, showing the train pulling slowly over the road and the guard closing the gates afterwards. *H. F. Wheeller*

CHAPTER SEVEN
RAILWAY TWILIGHT

THROUGHOUT the uneasy years leading up to the outbreak of the Second World War, the Southern maintained a summer service of half a dozen trains each way on weekdays with four trips on Sundays. At holiday periods these were augmented, sometimes to as many as eleven trains each way. Nevertheless, following the abolition of ferry tolls in 1929 and the rising tide of road traffic, the gradual sapping of the railway's regular lifeblood continued throughout the 'thirties.

During the autumn and winter of 1937 there were two more incidents on the branch which are worth recording. On Tuesday, 19th October, the 7.55pm from Leysdown ran into one of the gates at Harty Road crossing. It was very foggy at the time and although the driver managed to pull up before likewise demolishing the second gate, he was subsequently cautioned for his less than attentive actions.

A much more dramatic occurrence took place on the 9th December when the entire 6.44am train seems to have had a lucky escape. Having just left Harty Road Halt on the last lap of the journey, the crew felt their engine and train jolt and then lurch to one side. However, it was still quite dark and nothing unusual could be seen. As it became lighter, a look out was kept on the return trip and to their surprise they found the track had been washed from under them to a depth of well over 2 ft beneath the sleepers. Somehow, the track had managed to support the weight of the train and its unsuspecting engine crew. Sixteen feet of the embankment had also disappeared due to the culvert failing to cope with the recent heavy rain. The two passengers on board were conveyed by 'bus, whilst the train remained marooned for the rest of the day. The engineering department quickly descended upon the scene, whereupon the service was able to be resumed at 4.04pm, although a 10 mph speed restriction was enforced.

Three days before the now-famous broadcast that Britain was consequently at war with Germany, the SR introduced emergency reduced services. On the Sheppey Light Railway this operated as shown below.

With the blackout regulations in force and with shields fitted to headlamps on road vehicles, it was necessary to act promptly following complaints that the crossing gate lamps at East Minster-on-Sea and at Brambledown were badly focused and difficult to see. Since both crossings were on the skew, it was almost impossible to adjust the ordinary lamps so that they were visible to both road and rail when closed across their respective paths. At Brambledown it was found that the lamp could only be seen from 30 yards when travelling from Eastchurch, whilst matters were little better at East Minster-on-Sea. The SR's Sighting Committee investigated whereupon, following their recommendations, 'ship's lens' lamps were fitted which much improved sighting during these pitch black nights. The committee also asked that attention be given to the wooden gates at Scraps Gate and East Minster which were begging for a 'much-needed coat of paint'.

Once again, Eastchurch became a target for enemy action and this reached a climax during the Battle of Britain, much of which was fought over the skies of Kent. During the month of August 1940 the daily attacks worsened, whilst the Luftwaffe chose the 13th as 'Eagle Day' when the concentrated pounding of RAF aerodromes would commence However, cloudy weather at dawn led to the sudden cancellation of this grand assault, but

The extent of the reduction in services may be gleaned from comparing these two timetable examples. The upper table is taken from the 1937 summer issue, whilst the lower reveals the emergency reduced services introduced on 1st September 1939.

some crews failed to receive notification in time with the result that escort planes took off without bombers, whilst other bomber crews failed to be escorted. A group of Dorniers continued with the sortie, flying around the coastline to avoid the Kent Coast anti-aircraft defences, before swinging into the Thames Estuary, intent on destroying Eastchurch. The RAF were able to successfully intercept them, but not before a bomb fell at 7.07am and blew out the railway track near the home signal at Eastchurch station. The 6.43am Queenborough-Leysdown was on its way down, but was terminated at Eastchurch once the marauding aircraft had gone. Repairs were effected that same day and normal working resumed at 4.50pm. Incidentally, it was one of these Dorniers, Do17Z, which, having blitzed Eastchurch, was promptly crippled by the RAF, but attempted to fly back to its base on one engine. Gradually losing height, it finally crashed onto the Elham Valley Line near Greenhill bridge where it broke up. Remarkably the crew escaped uninjured, but were promptly arrested by the Barham Division of the Home Guard.

Two days later, at four in the afternoon, the Luftwaffe returned for another go, this time dropping a bomb which overshot the mark and instead blew another great hole in the track at Eastchurch station, demolishing the level crossing gates in the process. Once again, the track gangs returned to make good the damage.

For a fortnight the railway was left alone until, on the morning of the 28th, another bomb fell next to the track at Old Rides crossing, but fortunately failed to explode. No one was aware of it until the 9.05am came thumping along the track and it was spotted by the driver who must have had rather a fright. All services were immediately terminated at Eastchurch until the bomb disposal squad had dealt with the menace.

The most serious incident involving the railway took place on the last day of that terrifying month, August 1940, when enemy aircraft suddenly appeared out of the sky intent on finishing off Eastchurch aerodrome. Once again, most of the bombs missed their target, one falling instead upon the railway where it completely destroyed a section of track and brought down the telegraph wires. Tragically, there were four permanent way men walking the lengths at the time. The men dived for what little cover there was, but it was an exposed site and they suffered the effects of the blast. Lengthman Hayward was killed, whilst lengthman Austin escaped with only slight injuries. Lengthman Fifield and relayer Waters were both quite badly hurt and were subsequently detained in hospital. At the time the 10.55am Queenborough-Leysdown train was on its way, but it was fortunately intercepted on the approach to Brambledown Halt. There were no passengers on board and after a while the locomotive crew propelled the train back to Queenborough. Following repairs, the line was soon re-opened, and a change in the course of the war meant there were no further attacks upon the railway.

The winter of 1940–1 came with a vengeance in the New Year when, on 3rd January, the Sheppey Light Railway was blocked by snow. On that particular Friday morning the wind was already blowing hard when the 10.55am from Queenborough bravely made its way out of the branch bay in the thick of the flurrying snow and darkening sky. The numbing cold caused the engine crew to try and keep as warm as possible as they made their way down to Leysdown in spite of the worsening conditions. There was never much time at the terminus in the six-minute turn-round period on this duty, but the chance for a quick mug of tea could not be missed, especially in deepest winter. At 11.36am the run back to Queenborough commenced, but the driving snow was falling heavier than ever as visibility fell to barely a few yards. So severe was the snowstorm, which was sweeping straight in from the North Sea, that the railway soon disappeared beneath a white carpet as the plucky 'R1' tank battled its way through blizzard conditions. At Eastchurch the crew were informed that the line beyond had become completely blocked, whereby a continuation of the journey could not be risked. As a result, the train was abandoned, while the service was suspended for two days until the weather improved. Gangs of men were duly despatched to begin clearing the line, the section between Queenborough and Eastchurch being open by a quarter past two on Sunday afternoon. Having released the marooned engine and stock, the train was taken back under its own steam to Queenborough. On Monday the SR was able to resume services as far as Eastchurch, but Leysdown remained completely cut off by both road and rail. However, further efforts to clear the line brought relief by three o'clock on Tuesday afternoon when the 4pm from Queenborough commenced a return to normal working.

In February 1942 a request was made for new copies of notices in relation to the working of the level crossings at Sheerness East and Eastchurch. The originals, which had been pasted onto the wall and obliterated by the painters, stated that it was the duty of the station staff to operate the gates, but the responsibility of the train crews at all other times. The replacements were provided in frames which could be taken down the next time the ardent station painters were due!

It would appear that this request prompted the operating department to review the method of working the line, which was viewed as rather unsatisfactory. The current arrangement was explained thus:

Special Instructions at Signal Boxes and Level Crossings: Sheppey Light Railway.
a. When short section staff working is in operation, Queenborough, Eastchurch and Leysdown are staff [i.e. token] stations.
   The personnel dealing with the staff are as under:
   Queenborough – Signalmen
   Eastchurch –   ,,
   Leysdown – Porter
   The Block posts are Queenborough, Sheerness East, Minster-on-Sea, Eastchurch and Leysdown.
   The signalling is by telephone.
   Sheerness East and Minster-on-Sea are not staff stations.
b. Fixed Signals:
   There are fixed signals at Queenborough and Eastchurch and a yellow caution signal at Leysdown.
   There are no other fixed signals on the branch.
c. Personnel:
   The personnel at all stations on the Sheppey Light Railway consists of one man. They cover the daytime and perform the signalling duties when the short section is in force.
d. When the long section staff working is in operation trains are not block signalled, the working is covered by the Standard Block Regulations, pages 77 and 78. It is really one engine in steam.
   With the short section working there is only the one staff and when there is more than one train following in the same direction the last train takes the staff.

In simpler terms, before any train could proceed along a single line railway, its crew had to be in possession of the metal staff or token, a physical piece of equipment that was handed between train crews and signalmen to prevent two trains entering the same section and risking a collision. However, since the working of the Sheppey Light sometimes required a second train to follow down in close succession, the first train was given authority to proceed by telephone between the block posts. The train following behind then took the token, but it wasn't allowed to proceed to the next block post until the station porter had telephoned through to check if the first train had cleared the section ahead. The LED Divisional Superintendent, Mr P. Nunn, concluded in a letter:

> 'It would seem that the whole of the instruction wants revising and if you [Supt. of Operation] agree that trains are to be telephoned between stations which are not staff stations, I will proceed on those lines and there seems to be no reason why this practice should not continue as it assists the freight trains on the Branch.'

A few months later, in June 1942, Mr Nunn wrote a further letter to explain why it would not be possible to alter the times of the trains to obviate the need to have trains running in close succession. One reason was that connections with the Sheerness-Sittingbourne line would be missed, whilst another was the extensive use being made of the RAF Depot at Eastchurch. He went on to say:

> 'I rather feel that as the present method of signalling has been in force for so many years, it is hardly worthwhile, at the moment, making any alteration. So far as I am aware, no cases of irregularities have come to notice.
> As no expenditure can be incurred in the way of signalling alterations, I would recommend that the present method be allowed to continue.'

As with the tragic incident at Minster-on-Sea in 1935, fate was about to prove this an unwise move and force the SR into updating the signalling system. Fortunately the incident, which occurred about eighteen months later, did not prove fatal, but all the ingredients were there for a minor disaster.

On 17th February 1944 the 10.55am passenger train pulled out of the bay at Queenborough on its way to Leysdown, comprising 'R1' class No.1709 running bunker first, with van No.2266 and the articulated set No.514. In the sidings nearby was 'C' class No.1682 ready to follow down ten minutes later, running tender first, with the goods which this day comprised three wagons and a brake van. It was a very cold and miserable day with sleet falling across the island, but nothing out of the ordinary happened until the passenger train had left Brambledown Halt. The whistle had been sounded immediately after crossing the road at Brambledown, where the 'new' board had been positioned to warn anyone up ahead at Newhook crossing that a train was on its way. Newhook crossing was clear when the driver looked out of his cab into the driving sleet, but only two hundred yards further the line passed over an occupation crossing at Old Hook Farm. All of a sudden there was a bang as No.1709 collided with a motor car which was across the line. The driver immediately brought his train to a stand, whilst the fireman and guard rushed along to the vehicle to try and free the injured occupant. In the general panic it seems that the guard forgot his duty, that of immediately placing detonators on the rails to the rear of his train to protect it. Indeed, the crew may well have assumed that the goods would have been held back at Minster-on-Sea. It was only when the driver heard the goods train hurrying down the line behind them that the guard ran back towards Brambledown, anxiously fixing the detonators on the topside of the rail as he went and giving the 'danger' hand signal as the goods train rounded the curve. By this time the guard on the goods train had spotted his colleague by the trackside and saw the train at a standstill up ahead. He therefore quickly applied and released his handbrake, intending to attract the attention of his driver. However, the driver had also been alert and was already making preparations to bring his train to a halt within a safe distance. The passenger guard explained what had happened before returning to his train which then went on to Eastchurch, followed a few minutes later by the goods.

The SR conducted an internal inquiry into the incident which it viewed with some seriousness. It emerged that, due to the bad weather, both trains had been running slightly behind schedule, the goods being held up at Sheerness East until the next section, to Minster-on-Sea, had been cleared by the passenger train. On arrival at Minster, the porter there had assisted the guard in the day's business as they were well aware of the need to be punctual since any delay had a knock-on effect throughout the rest of the day to other, connecting, services. The porter had then gone off, in the normal way, to telephone Eastchurch station to find out if the passenger train was 'out of section'. However, Eastchurch replied that the train hadn't arrived. Intending to tell the goods train crew that they'd be delayed yet further, the dismay felt can easily be imagined when the porter went outside only to see the train had already steamed off into the distance.

Subsequently, the goods guard was severely reprimanded for starting away without receiving authority from the porter at Minster-on-Sea that it was safe to do so. The passenger guard was also heavily criticised for only protecting his train after the goods train had been heard. The signalman at Eastchurch and the temporary porter at Minster were also cautioned for failing to report to the station master at Queenborough that the passenger train had been an unduly long time in section. Neither had the fact that the goods train had gone ahead without permission been reported.

Clearly, the Southern Railway could not allow the somewhat archaic method of signalling on the Sheppey Light Railway to continue. The demands being made on the branch had exceeded the original mode of working which, in fairness, had proved to be reliable and satisfactory. The strains of handling extra wartime traffic and interlocking the branch line's services into the more-intensive mainland schedules were beginning to show.

Initially, it was proposed to abolish the block posts at Sheerness East and Minster-on-Sea, the system which had caused the recent irregularity. However, the wartime RAF traffic then being dealt with at Eastchurch precluded any move in this direction. It was also found that any attempt to revise the timetable would result in the breaking of valuable connections. Labour was drawn from the districts served by the Leysdown branch, which maintained the considerable industrial activity in Queenborough and Sheerness. Nothing, it was agreed, could be allowed to interfere with the war effort. Since it transpired that the SR had every hope of seeing the area revert to its former popularity once the war was over, significant improvements were authorised. Costing £418, these included the provision of starting signals in each direction at Minster-on-Sea and Sheerness East stations. These were modern, rail-built, upper quadrant semaphores, which looked a little out of place on the rustic backwater of the old Sheppey Light. Expensive interlocking with the gates was not thought necessary, so train crews would need to be alert at all times. Both installations were brought into use as from 24th April 1945. At Sheerness East the new starting signal for the Queenborough direction had to be placed on the 'wrong' side of the line, i.e. to the right of the track. The reason behind this was that the civil engineer was against disturbing the earth buffer

Familiar High Street names such as the Co-op, Woolworths and Hovis are displayed here in this appealing view taken many summers ago. The abundance of shop blinds is quite striking. These not only protected the wide variety of goods on show from the fierce heat and light of the midday sun, but also provided welcome shade for the passer-by.

Collection Richard Cullen

An 'R' class No. 1673, in very drab postwar condition, resting at Leysdown with an afternoon service during 1949.
Dr. P. Ransome-Wallis/National Railway Museum

stops on the intended site, partly due to a shortage of labour, but mostly the pressure of work generally.

The return to more peaceful days unfortunately brought little reward for the railway. The eventual loss of valuable business connected with the RAF was not compensated by the expected rise in ordinary passenger traffic. In August 1945, the *Sheerness Times* reported 'the largest crowds since 1939' over the Bank Holiday period. 'Buses to Leysdown and other parts of the island were packed solid' it continued, but unfortunately the same could not be said of the few trains which meandered through those soft and yellow, ripening fields of harvest time. There was now only a service of four trains each way on weekdays, whilst on Sundays, the most popular day for getting out and about, the rails remained silent.

In the years leading up to the nationalisation of the railways there was much talk of a truly integrated transport system, and everyone held out great hopes for the future of the industry. Indeed, some quite grand and remarkable schemes were put forward to the Southern Railway and its successor, the Southern Region of British Railways, for improving rail access to Sheppey. Local councillors were much in favour of the idea of having a tunnel underneath the Swale, but it is hardly surprising to learn that this was deemed too costly. More serious thought was given to making greater use of the Sittingbourne West Loop, which provided direct access between Sheppey and London. However, this idea, as well as the hope to see the Sittingbourne-Sheerness line doubled throughout, were eventually dropped.

It is also worth mentioning that Mr George Ramuz was still actively thinking about the development of the island, even though his grand schemes for Minster during the days before the Great War had virtually come to nothing. He suggested that a Medway tunnel be constructed, between Port Victoria and Sheerness. This would enable the island to be connected to the shortest possible rail route by utilising the Hundred of Hoo line. High capital cost against a projected meagre financial return obviously prevented anyone taking the idea seriously, but it serves as one of the more interesting armchair pipe dreams.

The drift away from the infrequent rail service continued over the next couple of years, its general inconvenience only serving to drive people onto the 'buses and into cars. The train service was also slow, the journey taking as long as it had in 1901 and often even longer. This was partly caused by the number of road crossings which prevented any speed being attained since the train had to stop every time to allow the guard to operate the gates. It was little wonder then that the line's passenger business became 'easy pickings' for the rival 'bus company.

Just as the tramway had suffered thirty-five years earlier, now it was the turn of the light railway to be cursed by impatient motorists who were forced to pull up while the train creaked across the road. This was especially the case at those crossings adjacent to a halt or station where a wait of three or four minutes was incurred. At open crossings it seems to have been something of a challenge to race the train among some reckless drivers who should have known better.

Collisions at the open crossings and running into the gates, where they were provided, continued in the somewhat time-honoured tradition on the Isle of Sheppey. On 13th December 1948, 'C' class No.1579 was returning to Queenborough with the 12.40pm Leysdown goods when it hit a pair of the gates at Sheerness East. There was no one on the crossing at the time and damage to the barriers appears to have been only slight. The station porter, whose hours of duty stretched from 6.20am-12.45pm and 2.35pm-4.10pm, was away for his meal break. Even so, it was always the regular duty of the train crews to attend the gates in his absence. Failing to pull up in time was no excuse and no doubt they were given a ticking off for not taking greater care.

Whereas on some occasions it was clearly the failure of the railway staff to carry out their instructions properly, in many instances they were blameless for the incidents which periodically

This 1930s view of Queenborough, looking towards Sheerness, shows the brick goods shed on the up side. The distinctive station buildings retained their somewhat ecclesiastical air.
H. A. Vallance

In this later view of 1950, the goods shed has been largely demolished, the amount of traffic in the sidings is appreciably diminished, whilst the station has a general sense of decay. The Leysdown branch can be seen curving away sharply to the right of the picture.
Denis Cullum

plagued this branch line. Such was the case the following spring when, in March 1949, the 11.36am from Leysdown was only three minutes into its journey when it collided with a van at Mustards Road Crossing. Although the locomotive received only superficial damage, the van was a total wreck. The train crew admitted they'd approached the crossing at rather more than the statutory ten miles per hour, for which they were subsequently disciplined. Nevertheless, the blame was laid on the van driver who confessed he'd seen the train approaching and had attempted to cross first.

An almost identical accident took place fifteen months later, in July 1950, when a train and van collided at Frog's Island Crossing. The service involved was the 10.55am from Queenborough, consisting of set 513 and parcels van S1353 hauled by 'R' class No.31674. On this occasion the engine was running bunker first and although the speed had just been reduced to a walking pace, the driver admitted he'd been momentarily distracted by some permanent way staff cutting the grass by the lineside. One of them had been using an automatic scythe with which he was having some difficulty and the driver was worried it was about to foul the track. Over the years the crossing had become partially obscured by trees and adjacent bungalows and outbuildings, so a clear view of either side was no longer possible. Just as the locomotive reached it, the 10 cwt Ford van belonging

This view shows Sheppey stock set 514 in the bay, and a train for Sheerness-on-Sea, comprising SE & CR 'Birdcage' stock departing from the opposite platform.
D. Trevor Rowe

The other articulated set, No. 513, waiting for a midday service.
D. Trevor Rowe

'R' class No. 1673 at the water stand at Queenborough in 1949. The pillar still bears its wartime stripes applied as an aid to vision during the blackout.
Dr. P. Ransome-Wallis/ National Railway Museum

'R' class No. 1699 arriving at Queenborough on the afternoon of 8th October 1948.   *W. A. Camwell*

Set 513 waiting at Queenborough with the 4.22 p.m. to Leysdown on 21st September 1950.
R. F. Roberts

Sheerness East in 1950, looking towards Queenborough and by this time appearing very standardised with its modern concrete platform and upper quadrant starting signal.
J. J. Smith

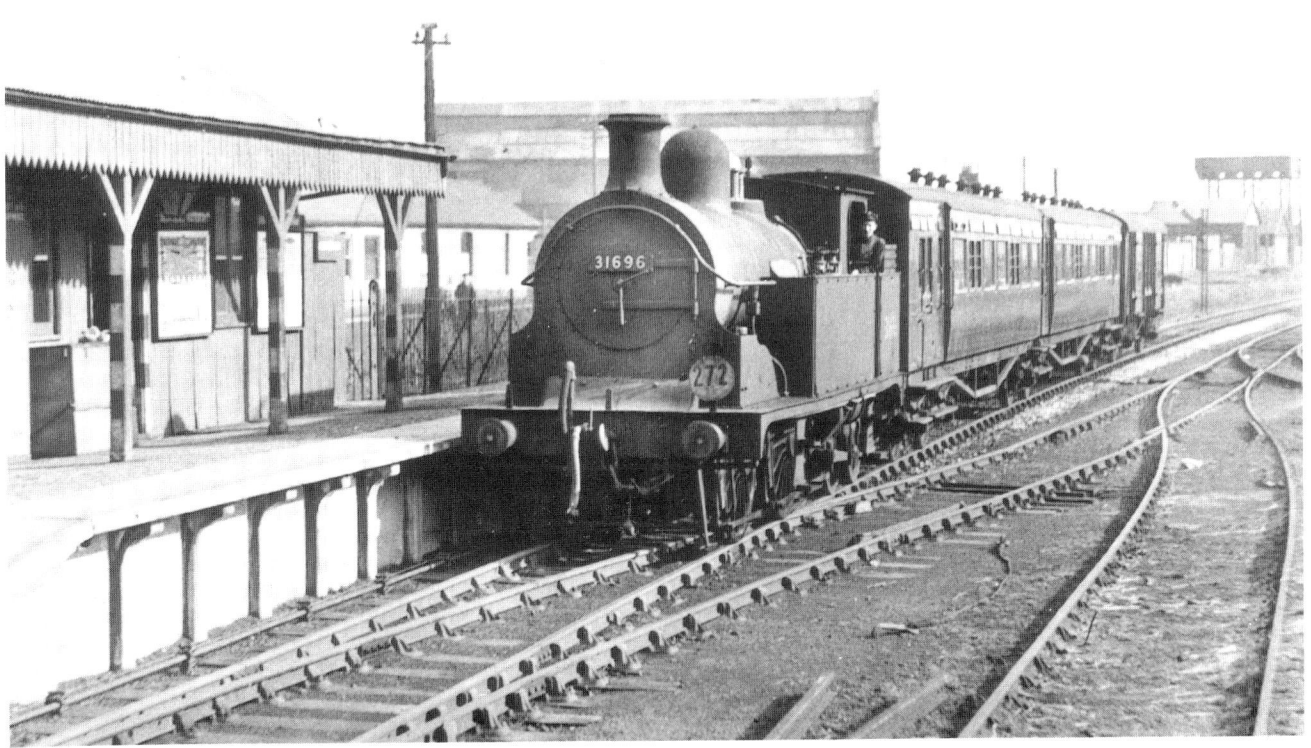
In British Railways livery and bearing a smokebox plate, this view shows No. 31696 sauntering into Sheerness East from Leysdown during the last year of the line's existence.
Dr. P. Ransome-Wallis/National Railway Museum

On 2nd December 1950, 'R1' No. 31705 with a train for Leysdown, pausing at East Minster-on-Sea. *Dr. Edwin Course*

to the Sheppey Mineral Water Company, suddenly appeared from the side, whereupon it was immediately struck by the engine. The van was almost completely overturned by the force of the collision which caused serious damage to the vehicle, but luckily the driver escaped with only minor cuts, although he was badly shocked. It was subsequently considered that the van driver had been at fault for travelling much too fast and without due care and attention. Even so, the Southern Region decided to issue instructions to all engine crews that every train should henceforth hold down the whistle from the board until the crossing had been passed.

Behind the scenes, it is hardly surprising that the Southern Region was scrutinising the receipts of the Sheppey Light Railway, in common with various other branches scattered across the south. Having recently closed another of Colonel Stephens' lines, the East Kent Light Railway, the board similarly viewed the Leysdown branch as surplus to requirements and a drain on resources. Gross receipts in 1949 amounted to £5,753, of which only £106 had come from passengers (including season ticket holders). Clearly, it had been the goods business which had been sustaining the line for many years, but even this was being drained away. With the establishment of the British Railways Road Services, Sheppey was served by its 'Zonal Collection and Delivery Service', based at Sheerness, a sub-railhead of Chatham. Although it was estimated that a loss of receipts would amount to £1,156, this would be far outweighed by a saving in annual running costs of £8,731. Therefore, the accounting department deduced, an increase of £7,575 in overall net revenue would accrue by closing the line. The final nail in the coffin was thumped home by reckoning that £28,000 would have to be

The guard on a return service to Queenborough unbolting the gates at East Minster-on-Sea to enable his train to cross the road. The bare elms of wintertime were once such a common feature throughout the island. *Collection Jeremy Segrove*

Minster-on-Sea station, looking towards Queenborough and showing the goods yard and siding. Coal seems to have been the only traffic when this photograph was taken in 1950.
D. Trevor Rowe

This splendid shot of Minster-on-Sea portrays the station in its last days and also shows the modern upper quadrant starting signals erected in 1945. The railway can be seen curving away into the distance towards Leysdown, whilst scattered around is a creeping tide of bungalows and sundry small dwellings.
Denis Cullum

An unusual view, taken from a train bound for Leysdown, running between Minster-on-Sea and Brambledown Halt. Again, the bare elms lend much to the atmosphere of this photograph and the island scene in 1950.

Dr. Edwin Course

Brambledown Halt, looking towards Minster, on 4th February 1950.

Denis Cullum

The waiting shed and simple wooden platform at Brambledown on 2nd October 1950. *J. J. Smith*

With the gates secured across the Queenborough–Eastchurch road, the 10.55 a.m., hauled by 'R1' 31705, is shown waiting patiently for the photographer to rejoin the train on the journey to Leysdown on Saturday, 2nd December, 1951. *Dr. Edwin Course*

A warm and sunny day with the village of Eastchurch slumbering in an age which, like its branch line to Leysdown, has long since slipped away.
Author's collection

Down at the station nothing stirs... The 'boys' from the RAF have all gone, leaving the brambles and buddleia to gain a firmer grip and add to the sense of decay of October 1950.
J. J. Smith

Right: From Eastchurch the railway climbed over the brow of a hill towards Leysdown. Due to its light railway status and special circumstances, the signals at Eastchurch were allowed to remain 'off' even though the crossing gates were closed across the railway. *Below:* The ground frame hut can be seen in the middle distance. *Bottom left:* A close-up view of the standard LC & DR signal and familiar SE & CR shunt signal with ringed arm which controlled the loop siding. *Bottom right:* A back view of the Eastchurch signal, looking towards Leysdown.
Pamlin Prints, J. J. Smith and Denis Cullum

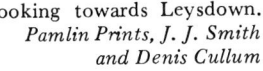

For some unknown reason, the Southern Railway thought it necessary to provide this very large green and white enamelled running-in sign to announce its presence at this desolate spot. With the railway disappearing into the distance towards Leysdown, there was very little else to be seen at this bleak and windswept part of the island. *J. J. Smith*

spent on permanent way renewals if the line remained open. With this evidence in front of him, the LED Divisional Superintendent needed no further encouragement to announce at the beginning of 1950 that the line would 'close down at an early date'.

Throughout that last summer there followed the usual calls for a diesel railcar as a way of making the line cheaper to operate. Councillor Richards said his council would 'kick like blazes' against the proposed closure, suggesting a petition be started, whilst British Railways should be told to reinstate the Sunday service – 'the most popular day'. However, not everyone was quite so upset by the news and some appeared to even welcome the prospect. For instance, the owner of the amusement arcade at Leysdown thought it would be 'a good thing' since the railway was, in his opinion, little used and more 'buses would be a better option. Unfortunately, though, for Leysdown and the rest of the island, the Maidstone and District Bus Company retorted that they'd no intention of laying on any extra 'buses to replace the loss of the railway. 'A very sour lemon indeed' commented the chairman of the Rural District Council.

On the 3rd November 1950, the Railway Executive announced that the line would cease operation entirely as from Monday, 4th December. Since there was no Sunday service, it meant that Saturday, 2nd, would be the last chance to ride on the railway that had tried its best to faithfully serve the island for half a century. The line received the usual dubious 'celebrations' as scores of people turned out to bid their farewells to the staff and the train which had seemed so much a part of island life. A reporter from the *Sheerness Times* went along to witness this final salute and summed up the scenes that Saturday evening:

EVENTFUL LAST JOURNEY OF SHEPPEY LIGHT
Local celebrities stage exciting mock ceremonies

OLD RAILWAY FRIEND BURIED WITH 'HONOURS'
PEOPLE COME FROM ALL PARTS OF BRITAIN

By the time these lines appear in print the Sheppey Light Railway to many people will be only a memory.

But to those who took part in the final eventful trip on Saturday last, there was a feeling of suspense and animation – like a kettle boiling fiercely with the lid about to burst off – for the farewell scenes touched new heights of excitement.

Intermingling with all the festive masquerading and mock ceremonial, some present felt an atmosphere of sadness in the thought that Sheppey, at the moment, was losing something, even if it was the infuriating, slow and easy light railway.

However, if the Railway Executive had seen all that was taking place and the interest and enthusiasm aroused amongst the inhabitants, it might have influenced them to have granted a 'reprieve' for a period – a kind of second chance for an old friend, the light railway.

'Well done, good and faithful servant,' was suggested as an appropriate epitaph.

The scenes on the train on this last journey from Queenborough to Leysdown and back again recalled those bygone days, when a relief train had to run to accommodate the number of passengers wishing to travel on the light railway, particularly at week-ends.

At each station people were waiting to board the train for the last time, and this desire spread like 'wildfire' throughout the area served by the railway.

LOCAL CELEBRITIES ALL THERE

The last train was the 4.27pm from Queenborough to Leysdown, returning from the latter place to the Borough. This proved to be a very memorable journey and history making, so far as this half a century old single-line railway was concerned. All sections of the

The terminus of the Sheppey Light Railway in October 1950, only a few weeks before final closure to both passenger and goods traffic.
J. J. Smith

Another view of Leysdown station, showing the whole layout.
J. J. Smith

community were represented and those not present can acutely imagine what the trip was like.

Members of the Sheppey Rural District Council entrained at Queenborough and occupied seats on the train. This railway had been operating in their district for some 49 years and they wanted to be in at 'the kill!' Amongst them were the Chairman, Wing Comdr. W. E. James, J.P., C.C., Cllr. Alfred Johnson J.P., Cllr. G. T. Parris, Cllr. W. Evans, Mr S.P. Walton (Clerk of the Council) and later they were joined by Mr E. F. Brading (Surveyor and Engineer).

When the train arrived at Sheerness East, there was quite a large contingent of passengers awaiting its arrival. Miss Olive Hooker was in charge of a party of merry children taking them on the 'Sheppey Light' for the last time, giving them something to remember and talk about for the rest of their lives.

Mr A. H. R. Copland, whose grandfather, the late Mr John Copland was one of the promoters of the Light Railway, was there taking in the scene and was obviously deeply interested in the occasion.

A similar story of people waiting at all the stations could be related and by the time the train reached Leysdown it was well loaded.

FROM ALL PARTS OF BRITAIN

One of the amazing features about this last trip was the number of passengers from different parts of the country, including Manchester, London and suburbs and other districts. Members of Light Railway Leagues, Spotters Leagues and other organisations were present. They were as keen as mustard on collecting souvenirs such as purchasing tickets of every denomination in possession of Guard Edward Cackett, who had charge of the train. They also, in relays, occupied a position on the footplate of the engine, No. 31705, and changed places at each station to give their friends an opportunity of travelling on the engine.

The driver of the last train was Mr Tom Birchnall with Fireman R. Pilcher, and Mr Edward Gill was the assistant Guard. It so happened that Mr Jack Buddle, who was the driver of the first train which ran from Queenborough to Leysdown, about fifty years ago, was a passenger on the last train on Saturday, together with Stationmaster W. H. Hall, of Queenborough. The latter had exactly the right approach to all the celebrations and was completely disinterested in all outside happenings.

He very much appreciated the good feeling and happy spirit which pervaded the whole proceedings, making his task a comparatively easy one, for there was an entire absence of rowdyism – just high spirited action with plenty of genial fun and excitement.

But the scheduled 5.5pm train from Leysdown gave all the passengers a wonderful run for their money.

A SOLEMN PROCESSION

During the day great preparations had been in progress at Leysdown in order to give a reasonable account of themselves. Rural Councillors and Parish Councillors, acted in friendly co-operation at the far end of the Island so that worthy recognition might be forthcoming as the occasion demanded.

At last the job of carpentry was completed and the 'box' was draped with black material. The coffin was borne on the shoulders of four sturdy 'mourners.' Messrs F. J. Purvis, J. Purvis, W. T. Rule and Sutchbury who marched in solemn procession from the village to the station, to the accompaniment of the 'Dead March' and the tolling of a bell. On top of the coffin there was a miniature engine, a guard's cap and a wreath of cabbages and 'mixed flowers', inscribed with the words 'In memory of the Sheppey Light that died through lack of puff!' Another wreath of garden produce was fixed to the engine and bore the following lament, 'I did my job for fifty years and can't get no extension; I'd like to have done it for fifty-one to have drawn the old age pension.' Messrs H. C. Love, E. J. Bonney, R. J. Loveys were amongst others present taking part in the celebrations. In the darkness, photographers mounted a long ladder to the top of the train and from the roof of the carriages took 'flash' pictures of the platform scenes.

There was a big crowd at the station and the excitement rose to a high pitch; in fact it was on the 'crest of the wave' as car horns hooted, fireworks and fog signals exploded, when the train moved out of the station.

The coffin with due care and attention was placed on the train and nobody was allowed to discover the secret of its contents!

CHEERING ALL THE WAY

At each halt and station there were people waiting to get on the train and at the 'gates,' waiting motorists sounded their horns giving a final rally to the slowly moving train. A large company joined the train at Eastchurch, with an improvised band. His worship the Mayor of Eastchurch, wearing his chain of Office (Mr Ronald Bigg) was accompanied by members of the Parish Council, including Mr Gordon Tomlin, Mr Bernard Bigg and other prominent residents in the village.

Mr Gordon Tomlin thanked all those who gave him valuable assistance in the arrangements including Messrs Purvis, W. T. Rule, W. J. Prior (Clerk of the Parish Council) and the Stationmaster and staff.

All the porters in charge of the stations were most helpful and considerate.

At the lighted windows in houses along the route curtains were drawn aside and the occupiers appeared waving their hands whilst doors were thrown open to obtain a better view of the passing train as it was moving out of sight.

At Minster there was another exciting demonstration when a second coffin, a highly polished one this time was placed in the luggage van by top hatted 'mourners,' together with a further consignment of 'floral tributes.' Sheerness East saw buses and cars held up at the crossing gates, and what a reception they gave the last train as it 'rattled and banged' over the main road towards its final destination at the ancient borough.

The fateful posters which were pasted up in the area during November 1950. *G. W. Powell, courtesy R. C. Riley*

The final farewell to a railway that had well and ably served its community for half a century. Here, 'mourners' attend with a coffin, while the railway crew look on from their engine, suitably bedecked with a wreath, during the evening of Saturday, 2nd December 1950.
G. W. Powell, courtesy R. C. Riley

THE LAST POST

There were further exciting scenes at Queenborough Station. The passengers crowded the platforms where the 'funeral parties' assembled and 'posed' for the Press Camera-men in various positions, some showing their handkerchiefs held to their weeping eyes and others with their top hats resting on their chests. After these touching and moving incidents, there was a move to the incoming platform where, after the coffins had 'officially' been received by Ald. R. J. Jennings on behalf of the Mayor of Queenborough a short 'burial service' was held when the funeral orations were given by Cllr. F. J. Purvis and Mayor Bigg, surrounded by a crowd of followers and interested sightseers. The 'Last Post' was sounded by S.J.A.B. Cadet trumpeters, under Band-master Cadet Officer D. Howard.

On the return journey a young Light Railway fan, Mr S. A. Fox, of 38, Exeter Road, Cricklewood, borrowed a railwayman's cap and made a collection for the Railwaymen's Orphanage which amounted to 34/7 for which they were very grateful.

This practical and good natured rag was a tremendous success. It certainly cannot be said that the closing of the Sheppey Light Railway, on the grounds that it cannot be run economically, was allowed to pass by unnoticed, unrecognised, unhonoured and unsung by Sheppey people.

What legends will be woven about the Sheppey Light Railway only the gods can supply the answer!

With the rails now forever silent, the following Monday failed to see the once-familiar train come rattling across the open landscape. On that day it snowed hard, burying the railway and the surrounding roads beneath a soft white mantle some four inches thick. In previous years such weather had never prevented people getting to work as the trains had always made their way through. Now, however, the 'buses and cars came to a slithering halt, whilst those that were still operable found themselves blocked in by broken down vehicles.

The loss of the line was sufficiently felt by the island community that the following week's editorial issued a solemn warning over the policies and attitudes which were then just beginning to gain favour. These words are appropriate today as they were forty years ago:

ANOTHER STORY OF LOSS
SHEPPEY gave a riotous farewell to the Light Railway on Saturday evening. The demonstrations which took place on the last journey were carried out in the best of spirits and with the co-operation of well-known inhabitants of the area served by the railway for nearly half-a-century.

All the masquerading and carnival atmosphere generated, the fireworks, hooters, whistle blasts and fog signals, were in commemoration of an event taking place which was symbolic of a growing tendency on this Island – that of losing something and nothing being added in its place.

In most spheres a story of loss can be recorded, but usually something follows or is established which compensates for the loss. Every flower, every bird, every beast, has a story of loss behind it in order that something better may stand in its place.

But this is not the case with the Light Railway. It has dropped out of the running. We have buried it and that is the end of it. For the Island it means a 'dead loss' and impoverishment.

There is nothing to take its place and that applies to many other things which have since been transferred elsewhere and once were established in the town.

The Light Railway has been closed because it is not a paying proposition to operate it. This seems a strange attitude to adopt where a nationalised service is concerned. We wonder if the mail services to outlying country districts had to pass a similar test, what would happen. It's just as logical for the Post Office to use this argument as the British Railways.

Only this week we have had an illustration of what is likely to occur in certain circumstances. Owing to the snow and frost and the treacherous state of the roads the buses were unable to maintain the regular services, consequently people had to walk long distances to get to their work. In cases which came to our notice people walked from the Oak Lane area to Glenwood Drive to pick up a bus for Sheerness.

Consequently, the Light Railway train service, which is now gone, was not forgotten by those people who had to walk to work. Sheppey folks do not wear their hearts on their sleeves, and last Saturday probably felt they had to blow off steam as well as the Sheppey Light, which was the rage and the main object of attention.

The obvious truth is surely this. That it is a case of the Island losing something, which, in plain terms, means less financial prosperity all round. Whether the contributions are small or great does not affect the general argument.

In the past we have lost the Gunnery School, the Wildfire Training Establishment, the Senior Officers' School, the Wildfire Baths, the R.A.F. Station, the Naval Stores Department, to mention only a few, and once again the story of loss is streaked across our sky with no corresponding sequel of compensation.

The demolition of the railway was soon under way in the following summer as gangs of men, stripped to the waist, sweated and toiled in the heat. The locality rang out with the metallic sound of hammers knocking out chair keys, spanners loosening fishplates and lengths of rail being hauled out. The rest of the equipment was removed, the station buildings demolished and the trackbed given back to the surrounding fields.

Today, a keen eye and a 'nose' for old railways might just be able to pinpoint the sites where village people once waited on market days for their local train with its friendly crew to come bustling along. However, even with the aid of a good map it is almost impossible to detect much of the line where brambles and thickets now wreathe those parts which the plough hasn't removed. Only at Sheerness East, perhaps, is there the tiniest hint of a former railway presence. Even so, it is difficult indeed to imagine all those trains passing through, the goodly assortment of engineers, contractors and workmen on that grand opening day, let alone the thousands who alighted from trams on their way to the 'Unknown Paradise'.

Many of the present generation and those to come may well grow up completely unaware of the light railway to Leysdown that so excited their forebears at the dawn of the 1900s. Nevertheless, the achievements of those individuals who so readily lent a hand for the betterment of this small island should never be underestimated or overlooked.

The line to Leysdown was certainly one of the more successful light railways, ably serving its community and bringing them a degree of prosperity and other benefits which would otherwise have undoubtedly been denied. Its importance to them and the role it played during the first half of the twentieth century should not, therefore, be easily dismissed in these more affluent and sophisticated times.

Sheppey continues to be looked at somewhat greedily by ambitious planners, but only time will tell if it will ever transform into a developer's dream, or an islander's nightmare. Is it too much to hope that, somehow, it will manage to hold onto what there is left of its secret, quiet corners where shady lanes would still delight the painter and those who might wish to wander aimlessly along its wearying, winding tracks? The bleating of new-born lambs across its soft green landscapes and empty furrowed fields is truly timeless, as is the breeze that stirs the waving corn and rustles the bending trees. Can we really be certain it is nothing more than the wind, or might it just be an echo of a long-lost train hurrying between those lonely wayside halts?

Leysdown station, 19th October 1950. *R. F. Roberts*

APPENDICES

SHEPPEY LINE—QUEENBOROUGH, EASTCHURCH AND LEYSDOWN.

To be carried out on Saturday, 18th, and Sunday, 19th January.

Alterations will be made in the signalling arrangements at Eastchurch and Leysdown to permit of the block posts at those stations being closed at intervals, as required, when the section will be as between Queenborough and Leysdown controlled by a distinctive train staff known as the Long Section Staff.

When the Long Section Staff is in use, no Train Staff Tickets will be issued, and the working will be under the "one engine in steam" arrangement.

When the existing Train Staffs (which will be known as Short Section Staffs), i.e., for the Queenborough-Eastchurch and Eastchurch-Leysdown Sections are in use the working will be under the Train Staff and Ticket arrangement.

During the time Long Section Staff working is in operation the down and up home signals at Eastchurch will be in the "off" position and when the change is made from Long to Short Section working, the signals must be replaced to danger after arrival of an up or down train as the case may be to enable the change to be effected, the relevant signal afterwards being lowered for the train to proceed; in this connection Rule 64, Clauses (b) and (c), must be carefully observed.

The Short Section Staffs are interlocked with the Long Section Staff by means of an instrument provided at Eastchurch. Both of the Short Section Staffs must be placed in this instrument to release the Long Section Staff, and vice versâ. The Long Staff must be restored to the instrument before either of the Short Section Staffs can be withdrawn. The withdrawal of the Short Section Staffs locks the Long Staff in the instrument.

The change over from Short to Long Section working and vice versâ can only be made at Eastchurch. The change from Short to Long Section working will normally be made when the 5.30 p.m. (N.S.) (5.40 p.m. S.O.) goods train from Leysdown is at Eastchurch, and Short Section working reverted to when the 6.45 a.m. train from Queenborough arrives at Eastchurch. In the event of any alterations being required, the Station Master at Queenborough will make the necessary arrangements.

The Long Section Staff working will be in operation throughout the day on Sundays.

The down home and up starting signals at Leysdown will be abolished, but to enable enginemen to locate their position, a yellow location light will be provided on the post now carrying the Leysdown down home signal at 12 feet above rail level.

The ground frames at Eastchurch and Leysdown and the intermediate sidings on the Sheppey line will be released by keys attached to both the Short and Long Staffs.

Ground frame "B" at Eastchurch will be abolished and the loop facing points, up home and the single line to loop shunt signals hitherto worked therefrom will, in future, be operated from the ground frame at the Queenborough end of the Station.

In connection with the above alterations, Sheerness East, Eastchurch and Leysdown Stations will be staffed by one man at each place whose hours of attendance on weekdays will be as shown below:—

Sheerness East	...	6.45 a.m.—12.20 p.m. 2.25 p.m.— 4.25 p.m. } (N.S.) 5. 0 p.m.— 5.25 p.m. 6.45 a.m.— 8.30 a.m. 9.15 a.m.—12.15 p.m. } (S.O.) 2.25 p.m.— 5.40 p.m.
Eastchurch	...	7. 0 a.m.—12. 0 n'n. 2.30 p.m.— 5. 0 p.m. } (N.S.) 6. 0 p.m.— 6.30 p.m. 7. 0 a.m.—12.15 p.m. } (S.O.) 2.30 p.m.— 6.15 p.m.
Leysdown	...	7.20 a.m.—12. 5 p.m. 2.15 p.m.— 5.30 p.m. } (N.S.) 7.20 a.m.— 9.30 a.m. 10.30 a.m.—12. 5 p.m. } (S.O.) 2.45 p.m.— 6.15 p.m.

The attendance on Sundays will be as required.

After the staff at the above-mentioned stations have left duty, the Guard of the train will issue and collect the tickets. Parcels traffic must be held back at Queenborough until the next morning.

If cattle traffic is required to be conveyed by the 7.18 p.m. train from Queenborough a man must be sent from that station to destination station to deal with it.

When it is necessary for the platform lamps to be lighted, this duty must be performed by the Porter before he leaves duty and the Guard of the last train booked to pass over the line for the day must extinguish the lamps.

During the time the staff are in attendance at Sheerness East and Eastchurch the Level Crossing gates will be operated as at present, but after the staff have left duty, trainmen must work the gates as shown below:—

SHEERNESS EAST.

	To be opened by:	To be closed by:
Down Trains	Fireman	Fireman
Up trains	Fireman	Guard

EASTCHURCH.

Down trains	Fireman	Guard
Up trains	Fireman	Fireman

The gates at Scrapps Gate, East Minster, Brambledown and Harty Road must be operated by the Guard as now.

During the time the Porter is in attendance at Leysdown, he will be held responsible for the running round movements, but when he has left duty the Guard of the train will be responsible for the duty, the Fireman uncoupling and recoupling the engine.

The work will be in progress from 11.0 p.m. on Saturday, 18th, until completed on Sunday, 19th January. Mr. Rose to provide flagman, as required.

SR signal instruction of January 1930 for introduction of long section staff working between Queenborough and Leysdown.

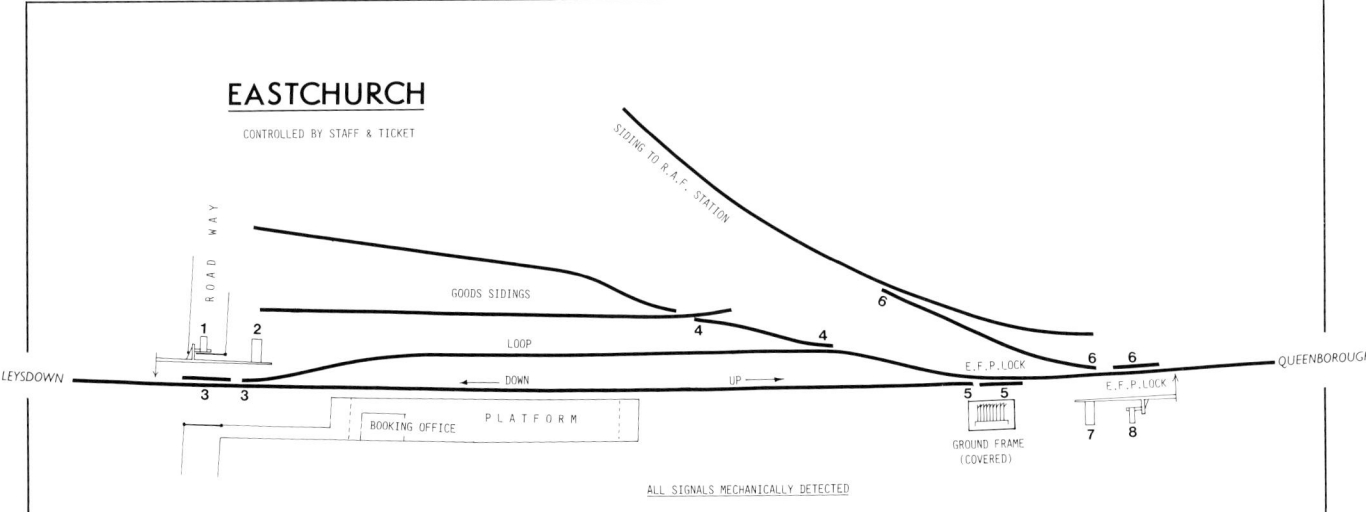

SIGNALLING DIAGRAMS

QUEENBOROUGH
- Sheppey Light -

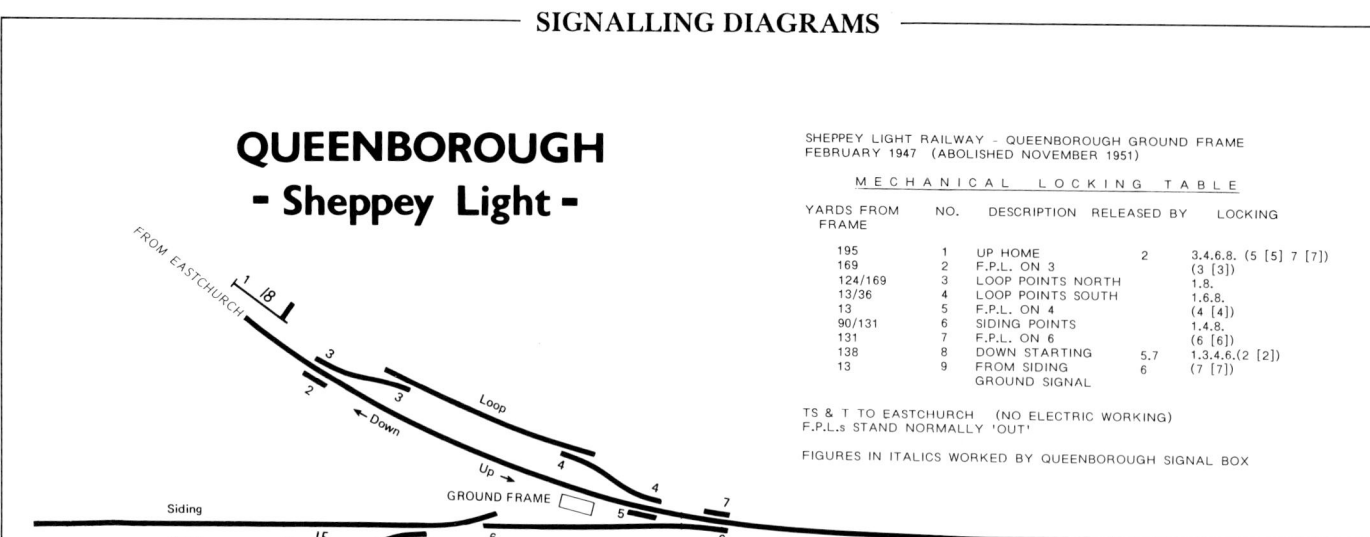

SHEPPEY LIGHT RAILWAY - QUEENBOROUGH GROUND FRAME
FEBRUARY 1947 (ABOLISHED NOVEMBER 1951)

MECHANICAL LOCKING TABLE

YARDS FROM	NO.	DESCRIPTION	RELEASED BY	LOCKING
195	1	UP HOME	2	3.4.6.8. (5 [5] 7 [7])
169	2	F.P.L. ON 3		(3 [3])
124/169	3	LOOP POINTS NORTH		1.8.
13/36	4	LOOP POINTS SOUTH		1.6.8.
13	5	F.P.L. ON 4		(4 [4])
90/131	6	SIDING POINTS		1.4.8.
131	7	F.P.L. ON 6		(6 [6])
138	8	DOWN STARTING	5.7	1.3.4.6.(2 [2])
13	9	FROM SIDING GROUND SIGNAL	6	(7 [7])

TS & T TO EASTCHURCH (NO ELECTRIC WORKING)
F.P.L.s STAND NORMALLY 'OUT'

FIGURES IN ITALICS WORKED BY QUEENBOROUGH SIGNAL BOX

MINSTER-ON-SEA

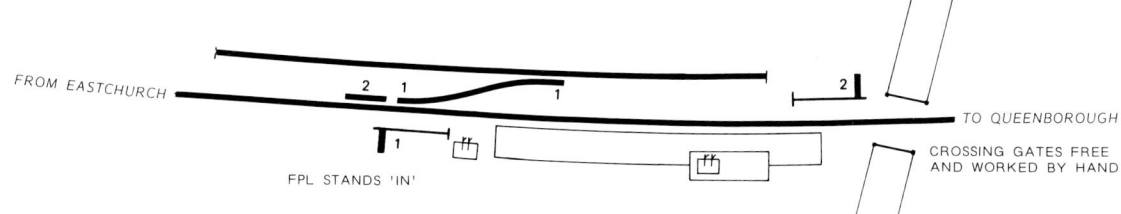

CROSSING GATES FREE AND WORKED BY HAND

FPL STANDS 'IN'

GROUND FRAME

YARDS	No.	DESCRIPTION
4 & 9	1	SIDING POINTS
0	2	POINT GUARD

RELEASED BY KEY IN TRAIN STAFF

BOOKING OFFICE FRAME

YARDS	No.	DESCRIPTION
80	1	DOWN HOME (PLATFORM STARTING)
30	2	UP HOME (PLATFORM STARTING)

NO INTERLOCKING

TRAIN STAFF & TICKET BETWEEN QUEENBOROUGH AND EASTCHURCH (SHORT SECTION)

TRAIN STAFF ONLY BETWEEN QUEENBOROUGH AND LEYSDOWN (LONG SECTION)

SHEERNESS EAST

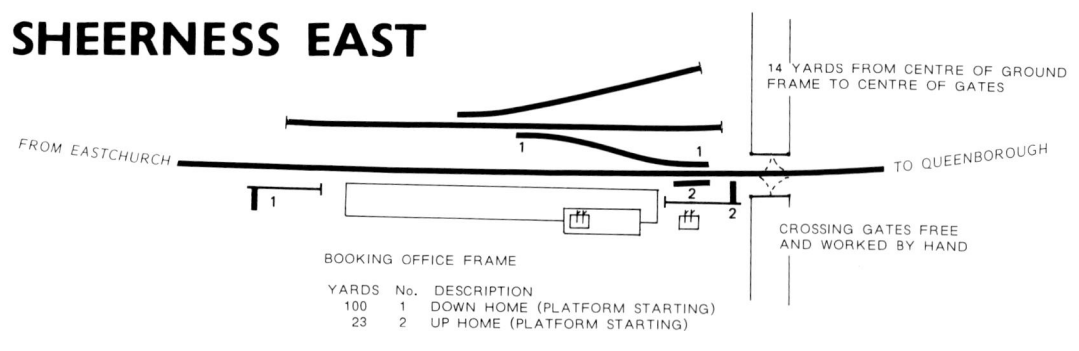

14 YARDS FROM CENTRE OF GROUND FRAME TO CENTRE OF GATES

CROSSING GATES FREE AND WORKED BY HAND

BOOKING OFFICE FRAME

YARDS	No.	DESCRIPTION
100	1	DOWN HOME (PLATFORM STARTING)
23	2	UP HOME (PLATFORM STARTING)

NO INTERLOCKING

GROUND FRAME

YARDS	No.	DESCRIPTION
3 & 60	1	SIDING POINTS
3	2	POINT GUARDS

TRAIN STAFF & TICKET BETWEEN QUEENBOROUGH AND EASTCHURCH (SHORT SECTION)

TRAIN STAFF ONLY BETWEEN QUEENBOROUGH AND LEYSDOWN (LONG SECTION)

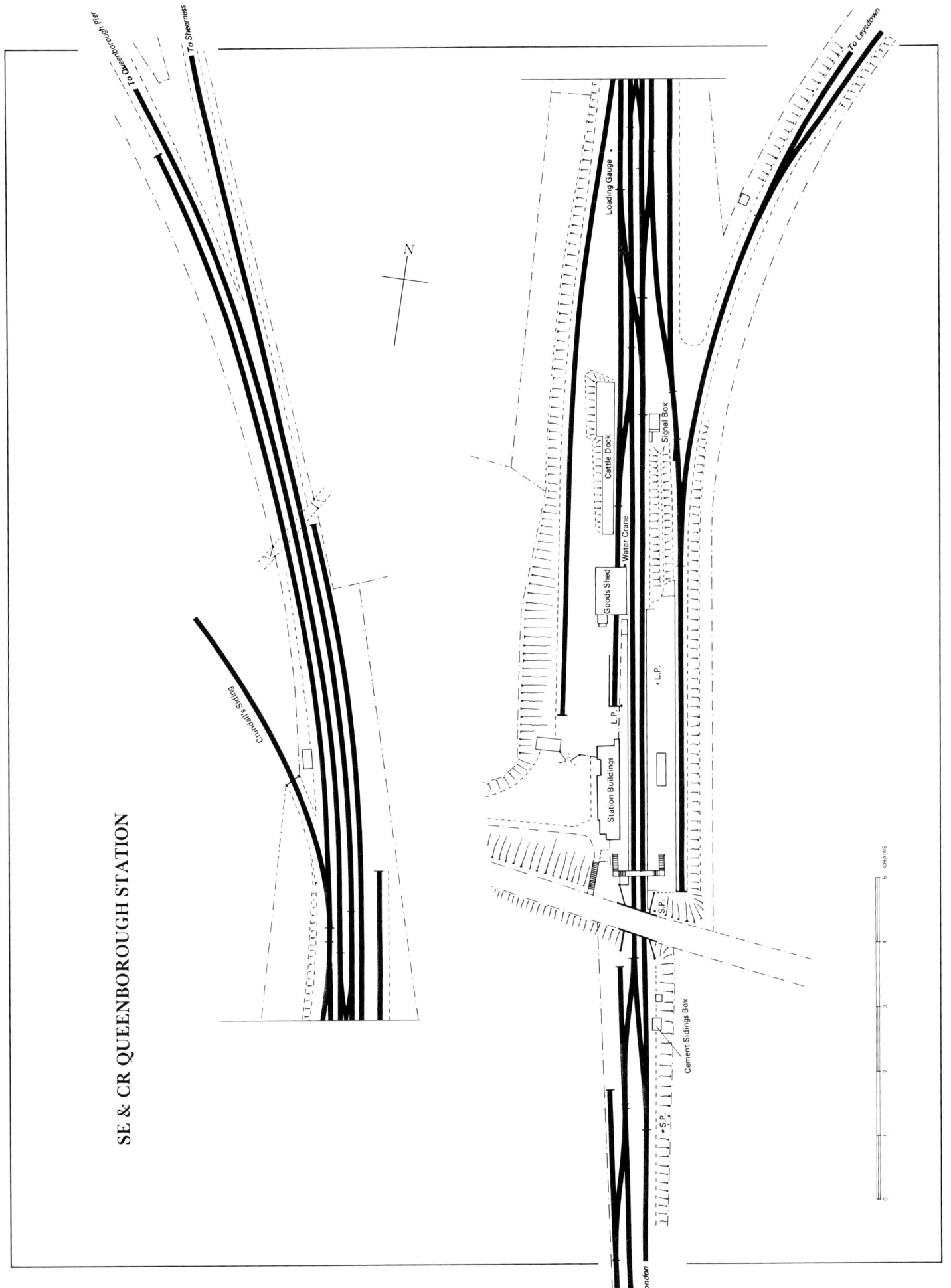

SHEERNESS EAST STATION

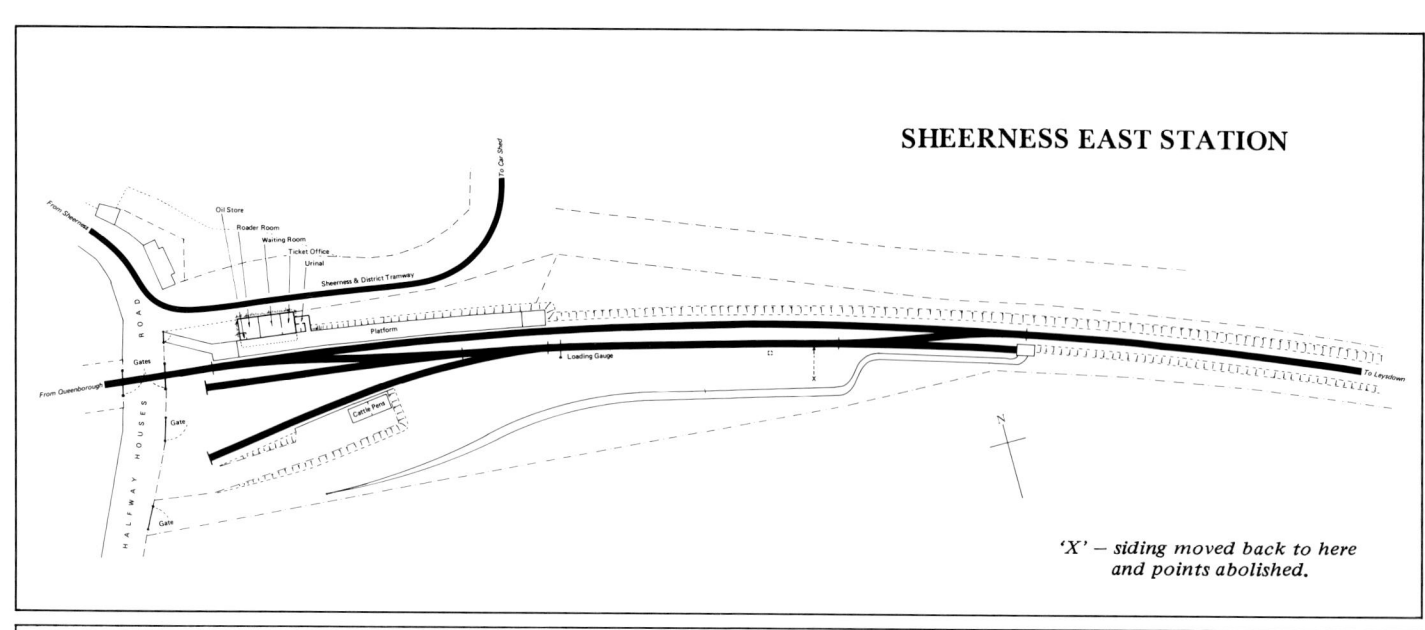

'X' — siding moved back to here and points abolished.

EAST MINSTER-ON-SEA

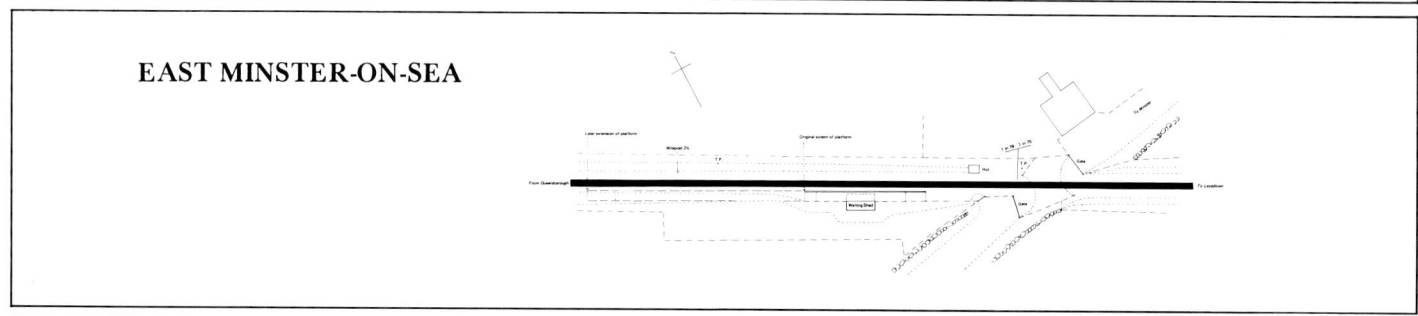

MINSTER-ON-SEA STATION

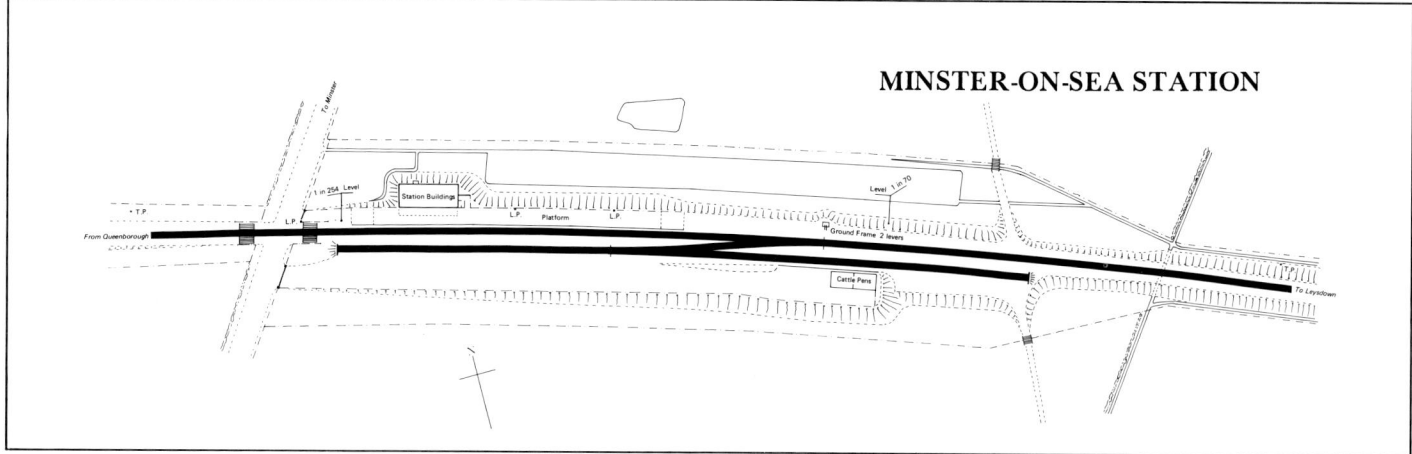

BRAMBLEDOWN HALT AND SIDING

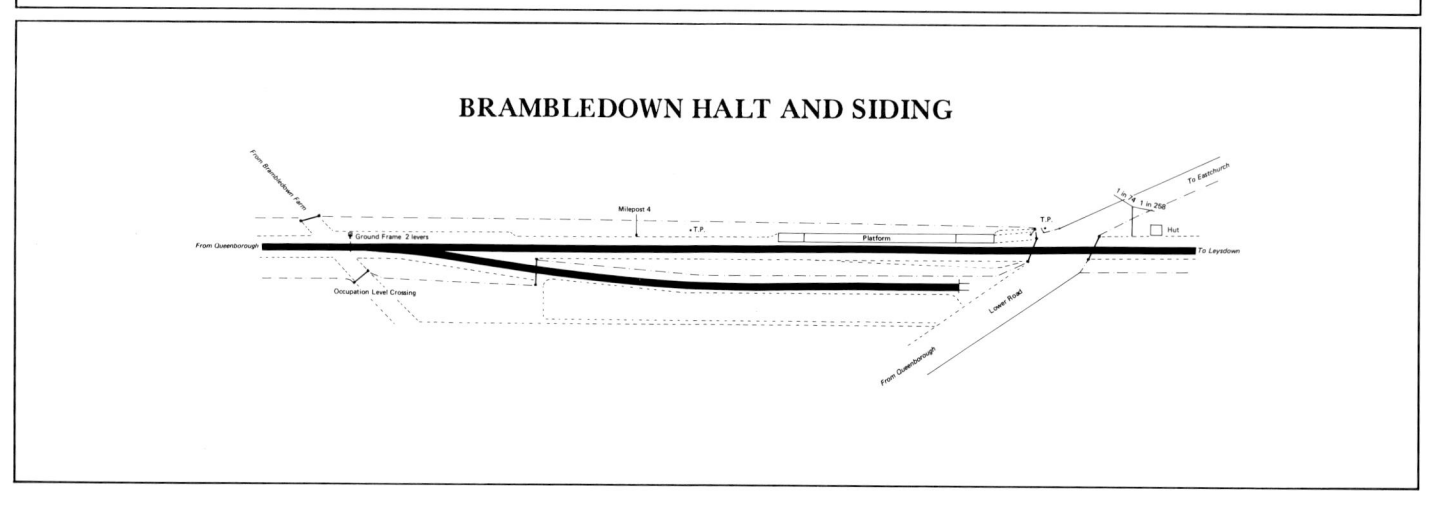

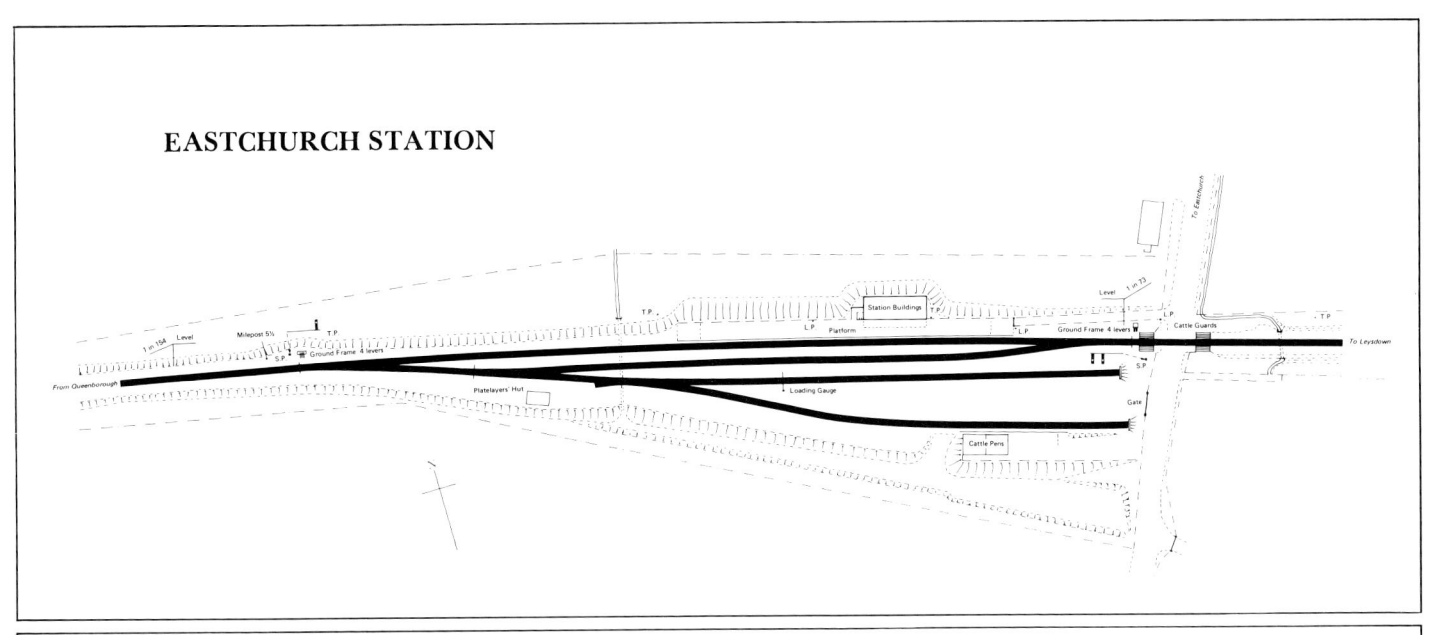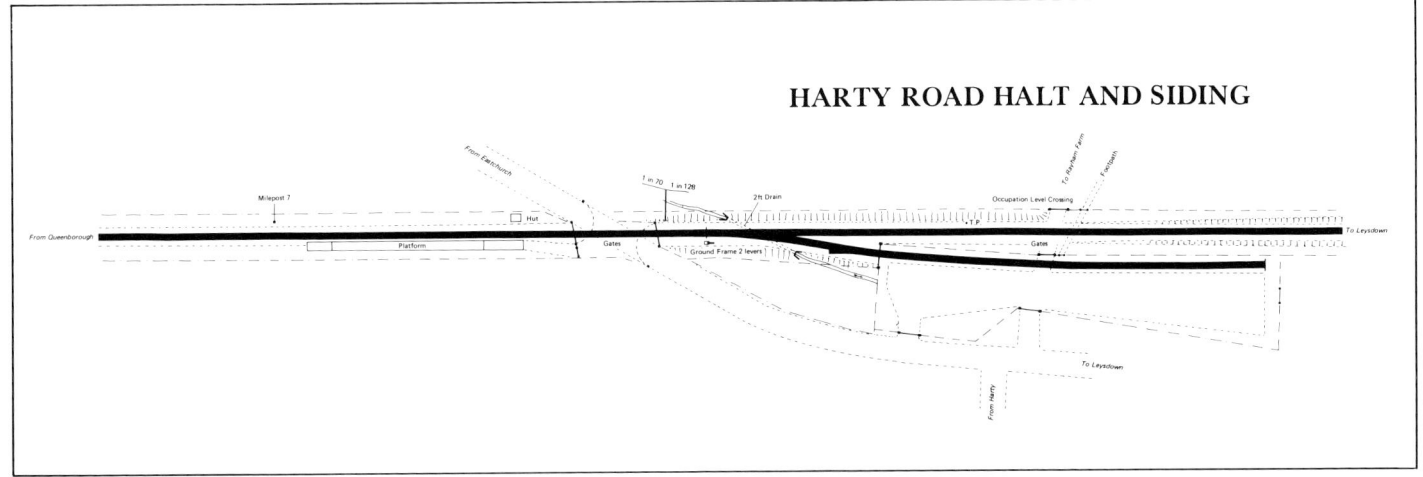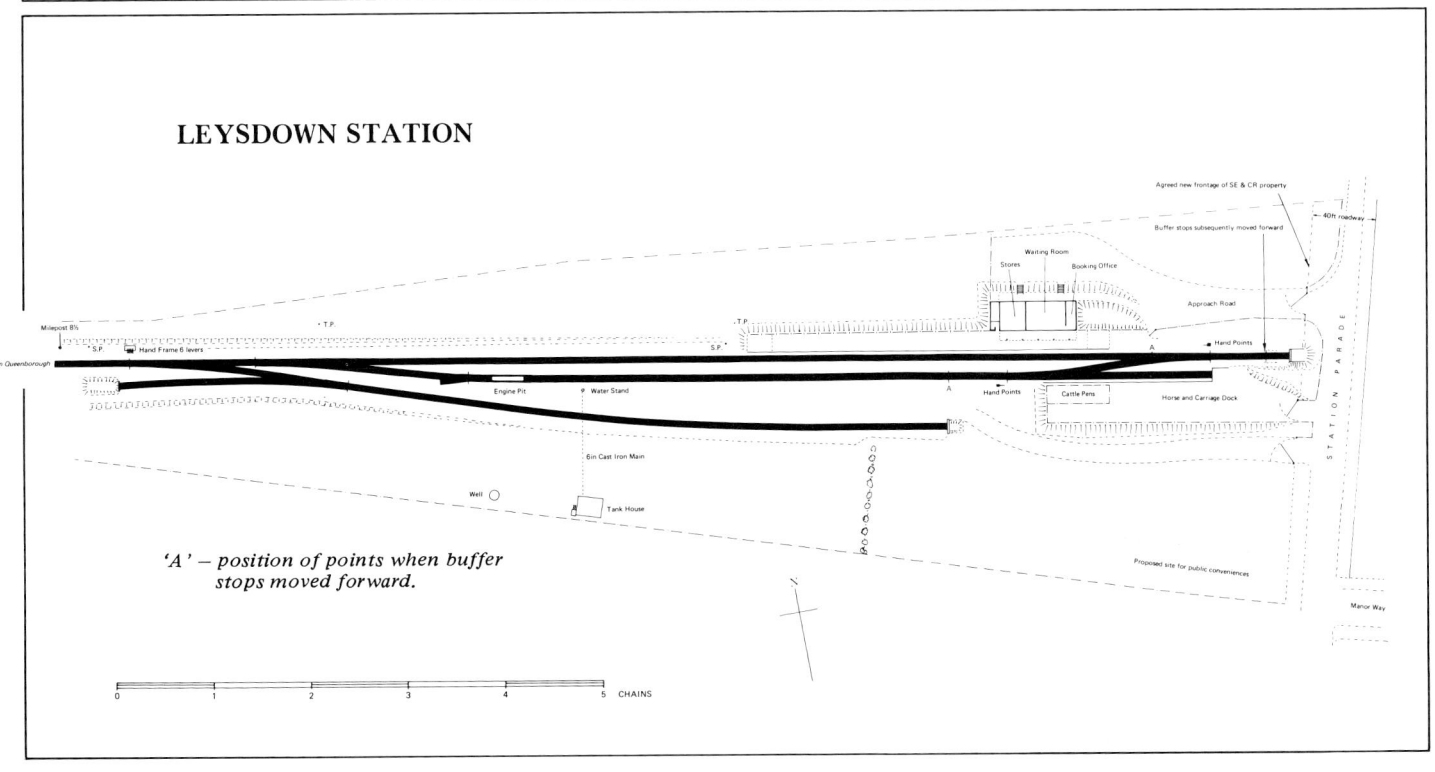

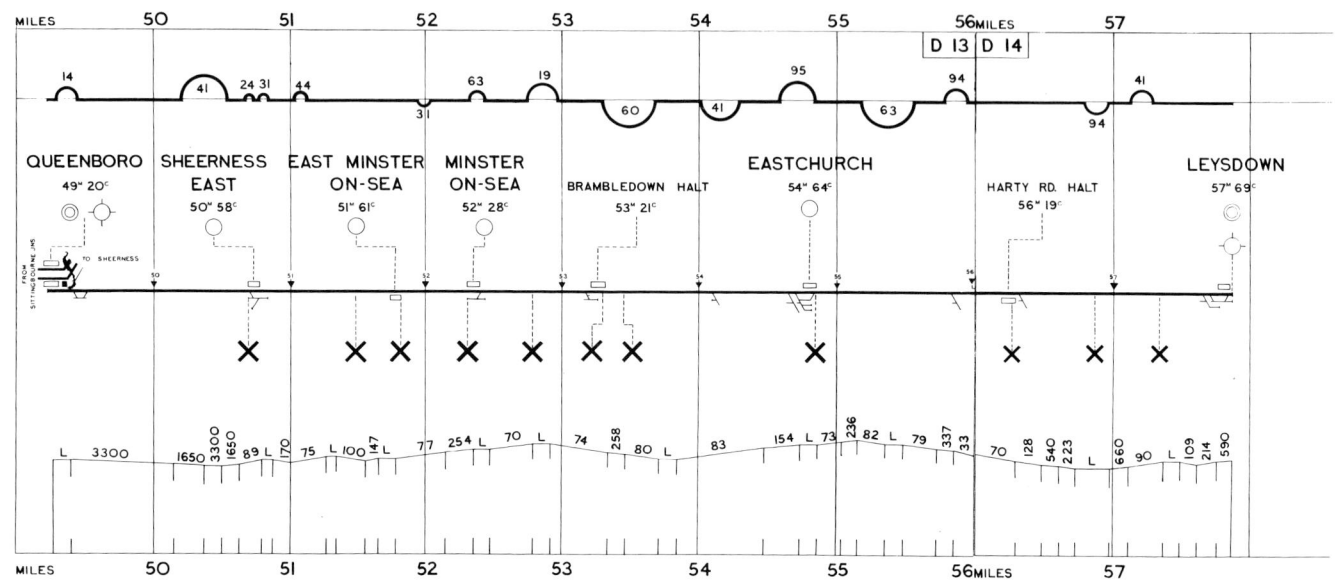

ACKNOWLEDGEMENTS

I should like to record my deepest gratitude to Reg Randell, to whom this book is warmly dedicated. To all my readers who have, over the years, enjoyed these books for Wild Swan Publications, I would like it known that none would have come about were it not for him. Reg not only encouraged me to attempt writing my first railway history, but was also responsible for introducing me to Wild Swan.

Next, I must express my sincerest thanks to Martin and Rosemary Hawkins of Eastchurch for allowing me to use postcard views from their collection. These have undoubtedly added much to the atmosphere of the book and enabled me to illustrate the story in the manner I so desired. Equally, I offer grateful thanks to Dave Gilbert who so enjoyed *The Hundred of Hoo Railway* that he promptly sent me his entire Sheppey Light Railway collection in the hope that I'd be persuaded to tackle one of his favourite lines! Dave has been very helpful indeed, as well as extremely patient, and I hope that this book will bring him much pleasure.

I would like to thank John Miller for access to material relating to Col. H. F. Stephens which helped add a personal feel to the line's early history. I am also most grateful to all those who have written about the Sheppey Light and were only too willing to assist, namely: Dr. Edwin Course, Peter Harding and David Miles.

Much 'behind the scenes' help was received from my good friend Denis Cullum who not only answered so many questions, but also took some of the best photographs of the line. Similarly, I am indebted to Chris Turner and John Creed who both assisted during its compilation.

To John J. Smith, Sid Nash, Dick Roberts, D. Trevor Rowe and W. A. Camwell, I'd like to record deepest thanks for venturing out all those years ago with their cameras in order to record for us the many scenes which have long since disappeared.

Numerous friends have rummaged through their collections to find suitable illustrations and I therefore extend my thanks to Dick Riley, John L. Smith, Jeremy Segrove, Bob Ratcliffe, John Meredith, Tony Riley, J. H. Price, and Mike Cruttenden.

I feel it is only right to offer posthumous thanks to H. A. Vallance and H. F. Wheeler who took some exceptional photographs of the line which we may all enjoy. I am also grateful to the National Railway Museum for permission to reproduce the work of the late Dr. P. Ransome-Wallis. Similarly, the Locomotive Club of Great Britain for Ken Nunn's photographs, the Gresley Society, and Pamlin Prints.

Thanks, too, to Sheila Judge, Barrie Clark and Norman Long who provided some inspiring recollections of the Sheppey Light.

Finally, it is with great pleasure that I record my sincerest and most grateful thanks of all to Paul and June of Wild Swan who made all this possible and whom I greatly respect. Their untiring efforts and dedication never fail to impress me and I consider myself very fortunate indeed, not just for being one of their authors, but one of their friends.